tagines &
moroccan dishes

hamlyn | all colour cookbook

200 tagines & moroccan dishes

Ghislaine Bénady and Nadjet Sefrioui

hamlyn

An Hachette UK Company
www.hachette.co.uk

First published in Great Britain in 2012 by
Hamlyn
a division of Octopus Publishing Group Ltd,
Endeavour House, 189 Shaftesbury Avenue,
London, WC2H 8JY
www.octopusbooks.co.uk

ISBN: 978-0-600-62266-6

A CIP catalogue record for this book is available from
the British Library.

Printed and bound in China

10 9 8 7 6 5 4 3 2 1

The Department of Health advises that eggs should not be
consumed raw. This book contains some dishes made with
raw or lightly cooked eggs. It is prudent for vulnerable people
such as pregnant and nursing mothers, invalids, the elderly,
babies and young children to avoid uncooked or lightly
cooked dishes made with eggs. Once prepared, these dishes
should be kept refrigerated and used promptly.

This book includes dishes made with nuts and nut derivatives.
It is advisable for those with known allergic reactions to
nuts and nut derivatives and those who may be potentially
vulnerable to these allergies to avoid dishes made with nuts and
nut oils. It is also prudent to check the labels of pre-prepared
ingredients for the possible inclusion of nut derivatives.

Both metric and imperial measurements have been given in
all recipes. Use one set of measurements only, and not
a mixture of both.

Standard level spoon measurements are used in all recipes.
1 tablespoon = one 15 ml spoon; 1 teaspoon = one 5 ml spoon

Ovens should be preheated to the specified temperature –
if using a fan-assisted oven, follow the manufacturer's
instructions for adjusting the time and temperature.

Fresh herbs should be used unless otherwise stated.

contents

introduction

In this book, the two authors share the delights and secrets of Moroccan cuisine through their own family recipes.

lemons, olives & argan oil

Preserved lemons and olives are indispensable ingredients in tagines, but they are just as essential as an hors d'oeuvre and can remain on the table as an accompaniment to the courses that follow. In Morocco, preserved lemons are made with very small round fruit, but there is nothing to stop you making them with larger, oval-shaped lemons (see page 18).

Delicatessens sell all manner of marinated olives mixed with other ingredients, but you can also prepare them yourself: simply marinate chillies, garlic, coriander and roasted pepper with the olives in the cool for a day or so to impart their flavours.

Olive oil seasons vegetables and salads and its fruity aroma lifts and enhances the other ingredients, but argan oil adds a more delicate touch, a nutty aroma, to a whole range of salads, in particular those using peppers. Tossing couscous grains in this oil gives a wonderful flavour.

the cooking pot

The tagine, a traditional rustic dish, is a meat (or fish) braise that mingles with the flavours not only of vegetables and spices but also dried fruits and preserved lemons (see page 18). The magic is performed by the lid of the cooking utensil, a round, glazed terracotta dish that lends its name to the braise. Shaped like a tall conical chimney, it allows the trapped steam to rise and fall, steaming the ingredients inside. It works on the principle of a braiser, effectively circulating the flavours and aromas. The tagine pot sits on a *braséro* or *kanoun*, which is also made in terracotta, but it can also be used on top of the stove with a heat-diffusing mat. If you don't possess a tagine, a cast-iron pot or heavy-based casserole will do the job,

for the secret of the dish also lies in cooking it long and slow over a very low heat.

meat

Lamb, veal, chicken, duck, quail and rabbit are the types of meat that work really well in a tagine. To ensure the meat becomes rich and melting, select your cuts carefully: too lean and you risk the meat drying out (this applies equally to meatballs). Using meat with a higher fat content means you don't have to add any extra to the dish. For beef, shin, shank or chuck steak are good choices; shin or leg of veal likewise. Foreshank of lamb is the cut of choice, but shoulder is a less costly option. Ask your butcher to bone and trim the meat, then cut it into large pieces. For poultry, use whole farm-reared birds with plump, flavoursome meat, and either cut them yourself or ask the butcher to prepare them for you.

vegetables

Onion, garlic and fresh herbs are the pillars of Moroccan cuisine, but the choice of vegetables and fruit for a tagine is determined by the season. In spring, the first really tender broad beans are cooked whole; later, they are quickly blanched and shelled. From spring to early summer is the season for fresh peas, green beans, courgettes,

wild artichokes and aubergines. Tomatoes, cucumbers and peppers come into their own in summer and, by autumn, it's time for turnips and quince. Cauliflower, celery, fennel and pumpkin are the winter vegetables. The vegetables of the day determine the ingredients in a tagine, as with the choice of salads that precedes it.

spices

The richness of Moroccan cuisine rests largely on the strongly aromatic flavours of the spices and spice mixes prepared by each cook. For example, ras-el-hanout is a mixture comprising up to thirty different spices: saffron, cumin, coriander, ginger, turmeric, hot chilli, paprika, cardamom, cinnamon, but also clove and star anise…

If you buy loose spices sold by weight,

keep them in small quantities sealed in small jars so that they don't lose their flavour. Saffron, always used in minute quantities, is found in powdered form or in threads.

dried fruit

The use of dried fruit in Moroccan cuisine, giving many recipes their sweet–sour flavour and unique character, is a Persian influence, introduced by the Arabs. Dates, figs and prunes find their way into dishes and their flesh thickens sauces and flavours the meat.

fish

The fish most used in Moroccan cuisine are gilt-head bream, mullet, tuna, whiting, sea bass, cod, pollock and hake, but also swordfish and red sea bream (pandora), not forgetting the indispensable sardine, the bounty of the Moroccan seas, which is at its best when simply served grilled. All these fish can be baked in the oven, fried, stuffed, made into fishballs or simmered in a tagine with vegetables.

couscous & pulses

It is tempting to use precooked couscous in a couscous dish. However, it's true that there are good-quality versions around and that they will save you time, the traditional method is also part of the pleasure of Moroccan cuisine, and mastering it is not as complicated as it seems. If available, use medium-grain, dry couscous (sold in bulk). As for chickpeas, don't hesitate to forego the soaking stage and buy without guilt a quality brand of prepared beans!

bread

To a Moroccan, bread (*khobz* or, in rural areas, *kesra*) is sacred and must never be squandered. All that is required is some flour (white or whole wheat), a little water, sugar and salt, a little yeast, and a light working (for the dough must not rise too much); then the loaves rest wrapped in cloth before being placed on a large baking sheet. The bread is shaped into flat rounds and has only one rising. Aniseed or sesame seed is often worked into the dough or sprinkled on the light crust. The soft interior is fairly light to absorb the sauce of a tagine but must be sufficiently dense to carry other food to the mouth, for in Morocco food is traditionally eaten without cutlery. Food is eaten with the thumb, index and middle finger of one hand, with the aid of a piece of bread. Flatter loaves serve to sandwich kebab meat.

fruits

In all Moroccan homes, meals end with fresh fruit. During celebratory meals, beautifully arranged fruit – piled on platters or sometimes on a bed of ice – is served in praise and celebration of the season. If fruit is prepared, it is scented with orange-flower water, dusted with

cinnamon, or strewn with crushed nuts. Indeed, nothing is more refreshing at the end of a meal than a simple salad of oranges or a pomegranate with a sprinkling of orange-flower water and a light dusting of icing sugar. Grated carrot can be served in the same way.

pastries

Moroccans end a meal more readily with fruit than a sweet pastry. Traditional desserts are fairly unusual, but something sweet between courses – milk rice pudding, for example – is extremely popular. Moroccan pastries are similar to those of the Middle East, but very different in appearance. Almonds reign supreme, especially finely ground. Icing sugar, cinnamon, orange-flower water, rose water and honey are very popular. Nuts, dates, dried figs, sesame seeds and, to a lesser degree, pistachio nuts play a role in the art of the pastry chef. And if these delicious morsels rarely round off a meal, they are the preferred accompaniment to mint tea, the ubiquitous drink in Morocco, offered as a gesture of welcome.

how to make couscous

500 g (1 lb) **medium-grain couscous**
1 tablespoon **salt**
1 tablespoon **sunflower oil**
500 ml (17 fl oz) cold **water**
40 g (1½ oz) **butter**, softened

Tip the couscous into a wide, shallow dish or tray so that it can be spread out.

Add the salt and pour over the oil, stirring it in with a fork to keep the grains separate.

Gradually sprinkle with the water. Let the couscous grains swell for 5 minutes, then coat your hands with sunflower oil and work through the couscous, lifting and aerating it.

Leave the couscous to rest for 10 minutes, aerating it occasionally with your fingers so that it doesn't stick.

Tip the couscous into the upper section of a couscous steamer and place above boiling stock. Check that the two sections of the steamer fit tightly together to ensure that the steam doesn't escape.

Make little holes in the couscous with the tip of a wooden spoon.

As soon as the steam starts to escape, transfer the couscous to the wide, shallow bowl. Sprinkle with a glass of water and aerate again, this time with a wooden spoon to avoid burning yourself.

Return the couscous to the upper section of the couscous steamer and repeat the cooking instructions in steps 6–7, then add the softened butter. Aerate the couscous with your hands again, incorporating the butter.

Again let it rest for a few moments, then separate the grains, mixing the couscous with both hands to distribute the butter thoroughly.

how to make pastilla

Butter a round baking tin or pie dish.

Lay 2 sheets of oiled and buttered filo pastry on top.

Coat your fingers with a light mixture of flour and water, stick 4 more sheets of pastry around the rim, leaving most of each sheet off the pan in the way that petals are arranged around the centre of a flower.

Lay another filo sheet on the baking tin and butter well.

Spread a layer of filling over the base.

Arrange the other ingredients evenly.

Cover with another sheet of pastry.

Fold in the 'petals', sticking each one to the others with the flour and water mix.

Finish with a final sheet of pastry, sticking it around the edges. Butter the surface well.

kemia & small first courses

preserved lemons

Makes **1 kg (2 lb)**
Soaking time **1 day**
Maceration time **3 weeks**

1 kg (2 lb) **unwaxed lemons**
250 g (8 oz) **coarse salt**

Wash the lemons thoroughly before soaking them in cold water for a day, changing the water two or three times.

Make two fairly deep incisions in the form of a cross in each lemon, starting at the tip. Open the cut as much as possible and fill with salt.

Arrange the filled lemons immediately in one or more preserving jars, packing them tightly and firming them down – it should be difficult to close the lid.

Leave to macerate for 3 weeks.

For marinated black olives, in a preserving jar mix 250 ml (8 fl oz) extra-virgin olive oil with 6 finely chopped garlic cloves, 2 lemons cut into chunks, 12 black peppercorns, 4 tablespoons of thyme leaves and 1 teaspoon of oregano leaves. Add 250 g (8 oz) black olives. Leave to marinate for at least a day.

prawn cigars

Makes **40**
Preparation time **20 minutes**
Cooking time **25 minutes**

1 tablespoon **sunflower oil**
500 g (1 lb) cooked, peeled
  prawns, deveined
2 **garlic cloves**, crushed
1 large bunch of **flat-leaf
  parsley**, chopped
1 large bunch of **coriander**,
  chopped
½ tablespoon **sweet paprika**
¼ teaspoon **cayenne pepper**
2 **eggs**, beaten
egg white, for sealing
10 sheets **filo pastry**
oil for frying
salt

Heat the oil in a large frying pan and fry the prawns, garlic and herbs. Season with the spices and cook until the mixture comes away from the pan. Add the eggs and quickly mix in. Remove from the heat and allow to cool.

Meanwhile, separate the filo sheets. Cut each into four squares and fold each square into a triangle. Place some of the filling along the longest edge of each triangle, almost to the ends. Tuck in the ends over the filling then roll up the cigar towards the point. Seal the pastry with a dab of egg white.

Heat the oil until a cube of bread browns in 30 seconds and deep-fry the cigars, in batches, until golden. Drain on kitchen paper before serving.

For meat cigars, first prepare the filling. Soften a finely chopped medium onion in 1 tablespoon of sunflower oil, then add 500 g (1 lb) minced beef or lamb, 1 teaspoon of ground cinnamon and ¼ teaspoon of ground ginger. Season to taste with salt and black pepper and cook, stirring, for 10 minutes, or until the meat browns. Stir in 2 tablespoons each of coriander and flat-leaf parsley. Add 3 lightly beaten eggs and quickly mix in. Remove from the heat and allow to cool. Complete the recipe as above.

fried pastries with goats' cheese

Makes **20**
Preparation time **30 minutes**
Cooking time **5 minutes**

200 g (7 oz) fresh **goats'
cheese**
½ teaspoon **thyme leaves**
10 **Greek black olives**, pitted
and roughly chopped
1 **egg**, beaten
5 sheets **filo pastry**
egg white, for sealing
oil, for frying
salt and **pepper**

Mix together the goats' cheese with the thyme and the
olives in a salad bowl. Season with salt and pepper and
bind with the egg. Set aside.

Separate the filo pastry sheets. Brush each one with
the oil, then cut into 4 strips.

Take the pastry strips one at a time and place ½ teaspoon
of filling about 2.5 cm (1 inch) from the nearest end.
Fold the pastry over and over to wrap the filling in a
triangle, then seal the end with a little egg white. Repeat
with all the strips.

Heat the oil until a cube of bread browns in 30 seconds
and deep-fry the pastries, in batches, until golden on
both sides. Drain on kitchen paper.

Serve hot, with lettuce leaves if you wish.

For baked pastries with goats' cheese, prepare
the filling as above, replacing the thyme leaves with
125 g (4 oz) lightly steamed spinach, well drained
and finely chopped. Melt 75 g (3 oz) butter and set
aside. Use 10 sheets of filo, cutting each one in half
lengthways. Prepare the pastries as above, folding each
pastry strip in half lengthways and brushing with the
melted butter before adding the filling and folding into
triangles. Place the pastries on a greased baking sheet,
brush with the remaining melted butter, then bake in
a preheated oven, 180°C (350°F), Gas Mark 4, for
30 minutes until crisp and golden.

refreshing salad

Serves **6**
Preparation time **15 minutes**

2 **tomatoes**
1 small **cucumber**
1 small **green pepper**
2 **spring onions**
1 small **chilli** (optional)
2 quarters of **preserved
lemon**, rind only
1 tablespoon **vinegar**
2 tablespoons **olive oil**
½ teaspoon **ground cumin**
½ teaspoon **mild paprika**
salt and **pepper**
whole **black olives**,
to garnish

Peel the tomatoes and cucumber and remove the seeds from the tomatoes and the pepper.

Cut all the vegetables and the lemon rind into small dice and place in a salad bowl.

Dress with the vinegar, oil, spices and salt and pepper and garnish with a few black olives.

For cucumber and mint salad, peel a large cucumber and grate it into a sieve placed over a bowl. Set aside for 15 minutes to allow the juices to drain. Mix with 3 tablespoons of olive oil, 1 tablespoon of finely chopped preserved lemon and 2 tablespoons of chopped mint leaves. Season to taste with black pepper.

spicy fekkas

Serves **8–10**
Preparation time **15 minutes**, plus resting
Cooking time **25 minutes**

1 packet fast-action **dried yeast**
1 kg (2 lb) **plain flour**
½ teaspoon **cayenne pepper**
½ teaspoon **salt**
200 g (7 oz) **Gruyère cheese**, grated
150 ml (¼ pint) **groundnut oil**
25 g (1 oz) **butter**, melted

Tip all the ingredients into a large bowl and mix well. Work with your hands, adding a little tepid water if necessary, until you have a soft, pliable dough.

Form the dough into rolls the size of a fat cigar and place on a greased baking tray. Bake for 15 minutes without browning. Allow to rest for 24 hours.

Cut the rolls into slices 5 mm (¼ inch) thick and arrange on a baking tray. Place in a preheated oven, 180°C (350°F), Gas Mark 6, and brown for 3 minutes.

For harissa fekkas, replace the Gruyère cheese with the same quantity of extra-mature Cheddar cheese. Omit the cayenne pepper and reduce the quantity of groundnut oil to 125 ml (4 fl oz). Stir 2 tablespoons of harissa (see page 76) into the oil before adding it to the mixture.

almond bites

Serves **6–8**
Preparation time **20 minutes**
Cooking time **15 minutes**

250 g (8 oz) **whole almonds**
500 g (1 lb) **puff pastry**
1 **egg yolk**, beaten, to glaze

Sprinkle the almonds with salted water and toast for around 10 minutes in a frying pan over a medium heat, stirring from time to time.

Preheat the oven to 200°C (400°F), Gas Mark 6.

Remove the pastry from the refrigerator, roll out, and cut into rounds using a 4 cm (1½ inch) pastry cutter. Place an almond in the centre of each, fold over to enclose, and glaze with the egg yolk.

Place on a greased baking tray and cook for 15 minutes.

For spicy almond bites, gently toast 1 teaspoon each of caraway, coriander and cumin seeds in a small pan. Using a pestle and mortar, grind the spices with 1 teaspoon each of chilli flakes and sea salt and ½ teaspoon of black pepper. Stir in 1 tablespoon of demerara sugar. Gently fry the almonds in 2 tablespoons of sunflower oil, stirring frequently, until pale golden, then stir in the spice mix and cook for a further 4–5 minutes to coat the almonds. Complete the recipe as above.

beef & gruyère pastries

Makes **12**
Preparation time **30 minutes**
Cooking time **25 minutes**

3 **eggs**
20 g (¾ oz) **butter**
200 g (7 oz) **minced beef**
1 bunch of **flat-leaf parsley**, snipped
pinch of **saffron**
100 g (3½ oz) **Gruyère cheese**, grated
500 g (1 lb) **puff pastry**
salt and **pepper**

Hard-boil 1 egg, then cool under cold running water.

Meanwhile, melt the butter in a frying pan with the salt and pepper and brown the beef for 5 minutes. Allow to cool.

Peel the hard-boiled egg and chop it finely into a salad bowl. Add the parsley, saffron, beef, cheese and 1 raw egg. Mix together by hand.

Preheat the oven to 180°C (350°F), Gas Mark 6.

Roll out the pastry and cut into 12 small rounds with a pastry cutter or using a glass. Place a little of the filling in the centre of each, fold over to enclose, and brush each one with the third egg, beaten, to glaze and seal.

Place on a greased baking tray and bake for 15 minutes.

For lamb & feta pastries, melt 20 g (¾ oz) butter in a frying pan and add 1 finely chopped small onion and 2 tablespoons of pine nuts. Cook over a medium heat, stirring constantly, for 4–5 minutes to colour the pine nuts, then stir in 1 teaspoon of ras-el-hanout. Add 200 g (7 oz) minced lamb and cook, stirring constantly, for 5 minutes to brown the meat. Allow to cool, then stir in 100 g (3½ oz) crumbled feta cheese and a little salt and pepper. Complete the recipe as above.

savoury aniseed biscuits

Serves **6–8**

Preparation time **10 minutes**,
    plus resting

Cooking time **10 minutes**

300 g (10 oz) **plain flour**
75 g (3 oz) **cornflour**
2 **eggs**, beaten
100 g (3½ oz) **Gruyère**
    cheese, grated
200 g (7 oz) **butter**, softened
2 tablespoons **milk**
1 teaspoon **baking powder**
¼ teaspoon **salt**
¼ teaspoon **pepper**
¼ teaspoon **ground aniseed**
½ teaspoon **sesame seeds**
1 **egg yolk**, beaten, to glaze

Mix the flour and cornflour with the eggs, then add all the remaining ingredients except the beaten egg yolk. Work rapidly with your hands without over-kneading, then leave the dough to rest in the refrigerator for 1 hour.

Preheat the oven to 200°C (400°F), Gas Mark 6.

Remove the dough and roll out. Cut out the biscuits with a 2.5 cm (1 inch) pastry cutter. Place on a greased baking tray and glaze the tops with the egg yolk. Bake for 10 minutes.

For aniseed bread, place 275 g (9 oz) plain flour in a mixing bowl and stir in a 7 g (¼ oz) sachet of fast-action dried yeast and 2 teaspoons each of whole aniseeds and salt. Stir in 1 tablespoon of olive oil and 325 ml (11 fl oz) warm water, then gradually add about 275 (9 oz) plain flour to make a dough. Knead for 10 minutes until smooth, then place in an oiled bowl, cover and set aside for 1½ hours, or until doubled in size. Punch out the air, then divide the dough into two balls, place on a greased baking sheet, flatten into rounds, cover and set aside for 20 minutes. Prick the sides with a fork, then brush the tops with egg white whisked with 1 teaspoon of water and sprinkle each with 1 tablespoon of sesame seeds. Cook in a preheated oven, 180°C (375°F), Gas Mark 4, for about 30 minutes, until golden.

beetroot & cumin salad

Serves **6**
Preparation time **5 minutes**

3 medium **beetroot**, cooked
1 **garlic clove**, crushed
½ teaspoon **ground cumin**
1 **lemon**, juiced
1 tablespoon **olive oil**
salt

Peel the beetroot, cut it into small pieces, and place in a small bowl with the garlic.

Season to taste with salt and the cumin.

Drizzle over the lemon juice and oil. Mix together and serve chilled.

For carrot & cumin salad, trim and peel 600 g (1 lb 5 oz) carrots. Cut them into large batons and steam for 10–15 minutes until just tender. Heat 4 tablespoons of olive oil in a frying pan and sauté the carrots with 4 crushed garlic cloves, 1 teaspoon of ground cumin and ½ teaspoon of paprika until the garlic begins to brown. Season to taste with salt and black pepper and serve drizzled with 1 tablespoon of lemon juice.

aubergine 'caviar'

Serves **6**
Preparation time **15 minutes**
Cooking time **15 minutes**

1 kg (2 lb) **aubergines**
1 kg (2 lb) **tomatoes**
½ teaspoon **ground cumin**
½ teaspoon **paprika**
½ bunch of **coriander**, snipped
½ bunch of **flat-leaf parsley**,
  snipped
3 **garlic cloves**, crushed
150 ml (¼ pint) **water**
2 tablespoons **olive oil**
salt
preserved lemon and
  lemon-marinated olives,
  to garnish

Trim and part-peel the aubergines, leaving strips of the skin intact, then dice the flesh.

Peel the tomatoes, squeeze them to release the juice, then dice the flesh.

Place the aubergines and tomatoes with the spices in a pressure cooker and add the herbs and the garlic. Add the water and oil, and season with salt. Mix well, close the lid firmly, cook over a gentle heat for 10 minutes, then remove the lid and let the 'caviar' reduce. If you do not have a pressure cooker, place the ingredients in a heavy-based casserole or saucepan as above, cover, and cook over a gentle heat for 30 minutes. Remove the lid and let the 'caviar' reduce before serving.

Serve garnished with strips of preserved lemon and lemon-marinated olives.

For roasted aubergine & tomato salad, prick 750 g (1½ lb) aubergines all over with a sharp knife, then roast in a preheated oven, 240°C (475°F), Gas Mark 9, for about 45 minutes, until soft. Cool then peel. Drain, chop and mash the aubergines well in a colander to release the juices. Over a low heat, reduce 500 g (1 lb) peeled and chopped tomatoes to a thick sauce with 4 chopped garlic cloves and a pinch of salt. Stir in the aubergines, the juice of 1 lemon, 4 tablespoons of olive oil, 1 teaspoon of ground cumin, ½ teaspoon of paprika and 2 tablespoons each of chopped coriander and flat-leaf parsley. Season to taste and serve garnished as above.

chicken & hummus wraps

Serves **4**
Preparation time **5 minutes**
Cooking time **10 minutes**

6 skinless **chicken thigh**
   fillets, about 500 g (1 lb)
   in total
2 tablespoons **extra-virgin**
   olive oil
grated rind and juice of
   1 **lemon**
1 **garlic clove**, crushed
1 teaspoon **ground cumin**
4 **flour tortillas**
200 g (7 oz) **hummus**
25 g (1 oz) **wild rocket leaves**
1 handful **parsley leaves**
salt and **black pepper**

Cut the chicken thighs into quarters and put in a bowl. Combine the oil, lemon rind, garlic, cumin and salt and pepper to taste, add to the chicken and stir well.

Heat a ridged griddle pan until hot. Thread the chicken pieces on to metal skewers, add to the pan and cook for 4–5 minutes on each side. Remove and leave to rest for 5 minutes.

Meanwhile, warm the tortillas in a preheated oven, 150°C (350°F), Gas Mark 2, for 5 minutes.

Remove the chicken from the skewers. Divide the hummus, rocket leaves, parsley and chicken between the tortillas. Squeeze over the lemon juice, wrap and serve.

For easy home-made hummus, put 400 g (13 oz) can chickpeas (drained), 1 crushed garlic clove, 3 tablespoons of extra-virgin olive oil, 1 tablespoon of lemon juice and salt and pepper to taste in a food processor or blender and process until smooth.

moroccan carrot salad

Serves **4–6**
Preparation time **10 minutes**
Cooking time **15–20 minutes**

2 bunches of **carrots**, trimmed
spray oil
3 tablespoons **sunflower seeds**, toasted
2 tablespoons chopped **parsley**

Dressing
4 tablespoons **extra-virgin olive oil**
2 tablespoons **white wine vinegar**
1 **garlic clove**, finely chopped
1 teaspoon **pomegranate syrup**
1 teaspoon **clear honey**
salt and **black pepper**

Blanch the carrots in a large pan of lightly salted boiling water for 10 minutes. Drain well and pat dry.

Transfer to a bowl and spray with a little oil, then cook on a hot barbecue for 5—10 minutes, turning frequently, until charred.

Meanwhile, combine the dressing ingredients in a large bowl and season to taste. Stir in the cooked carrots, sunflower seeds and parsley and toss well. Serve hot.

For spiced carrot salad, mix 450 g (14½ oz) peeled and roughly grated carrots with the chopped flesh of 2 oranges. Make a dressing from 2 tablespoons of orange juice, 1 tablespoon of lemon juice, 2 tablespoons of olive oil, 1 teaspoon of sugar and ½ teaspoon each of ground cumin and cinnamon. Season to taste with salt and black pepper. Toss the carrot and orange mixture in the dressing, then stir in a handful of chopped coriander. Garnish with coriander sprigs to serve.

roasted peppers with argan oil

Serves **6**
Preparation time **5 minutes**
Cooking time **20 minutes**

6 large **red peppers**
3 **garlic cloves**, cut into
  tiny pieces
1 **lemon**, juiced
½ teaspoon **ground cumin**
2 tablespoons **argan oil**
salt

Preheat the grill and roast the peppers, turning until the skin starts to blacken on all sides.

Remove from the heat and put in a polythene bag to cool. Once cool, remove the skins and seeds. Cut the flesh into pieces.

Put the peppers in a bowl and mix with the garlic, lemon juice, cumin, oil and salt to taste. Serve cold.

For roasted pepper & chickpea salad, prepare 4 large red peppers as above. Mix a 400 g (13 oz) can of chickpeas, rinsed and drained, with 2 crushed garlic cloves, the juice of 1 lemon and 3 tablespoons of olive oil. Add 1 teaspoon of chopped oregano, season to taste with salt and black pepper and mix well. Gently fold in the peppers.

roasted peppers with lemon

Serves **6**
Preparation time **5 minutes**
Cooking time **20 minutes**

6 large **green peppers**
3 **garlic cloves**, cut into tiny
   pieces
1 **lemon**, juiced
½ teaspoon **ground cumin**
2 tablespoons **olive oil**
salt

Preheat the grill and roast the peppers, turning until the skin starts to blacken on all sides.

Remove from the heat and put in a polythene bag to cool. Once cool, remove the skins and seeds. Cut the flesh into pieces.

Put the peppers in a bowl and mix with the garlic, lemon juice, cumin, oil and salt to taste. Serve cold.

For red pepper dip, prepare 6 red peppers as above. Blend the chopped peppers to a purée in a food processor with 2 crushed garlic cloves, the juice of 1½ lemons, 1 teaspoon of ground cumin, a pinch of chilli pepper, 4 tablespoons of olive oil and salt to taste. To serve, stir 2 tablespoons each of chopped coriander and flat-leaf parsley into the dip with the chopped peel of ½ a preserved lemon.

roasted pepper & tomato salad

Serves **6**
Preparation time **10 minutes**
Cooking time **20 minutes**

500 g (1 lb) **green peppers**
½ **preserved lemon**
1 kg (2 lb) **tomatoes**
3 tablespoons **olive oil**
salt

Preheat the grill and roast the peppers, turning until the skin starts to blacken on all sides.

Remove from the heat and put in a polythene bag to cool. Once cool, remove the skins and seeds.

Meanwhile, soak the preserved lemon in warm water for 5 minutes to remove the salt.

Peel the tomatoes, remove the seeds and juice, and cut the flesh into slices.

Cut the peppers into long slices and add the tomatoes and the preserved lemon, cut into tiny pieces. Dress with the oil and salt to taste.

For tomatoes stuffed with roasted peppers, prepare 4 red peppers as above and cut them into fine strips. Mix with 4 tablespoons of chopped black olives, 1 tablespoon of toasted pine nuts, the chopped peel of ½ a preserved lemon and 2 tablespoons each of capers and chopped flat-leaf parsley. Cut the tops off 6 large tomatoes, then scoop out the centres and seeds with a teaspoon. Fill with the roasted pepper mixture, replace the tops and bake in an oiled ovenproof dish in a preheated oven, 180°C (350°F), Gas Mark 4, for about 20 minutes, until softened.

crispy lamb moroccan rolls

Serves **2**
Preparation time **15 minutes**
Cooking time **10 minutes**

250 g (8 oz) **minced lamb**
1 teaspoon **ground cinnamon**
3 tablespoons **pine nuts**
2 **naan breads**, warmed
200 g (7 oz) **hummus**
2 tablespoons **mint leaves**
1 **Little Gem lettuce**, finely
    shredded (optional)

Fry the minced lamb in a large, nonstick frying pan for 8–10 minutes until it becomes golden brown. Add the cinnamon and pine nuts and cook again for 1 minute. Remove from the heat.

Place the warm naan breads on a chopping board and, using a rolling pin, firmly roll to flatten.

Mix the hummus with half the mint leaves, then spread in a thick layer over the warmed naans. Spoon over the crispy lamb, then scatter over the shredded lettuce, if using, and the remaining mint leaves. Tightly roll up and secure with cocktail sticks.

Serve immediately.

For lamb kofta, mix the raw minced lamb with 4 finely chopped spring onions, 1 teaspoon of ground cinnamon, a very finely chopped tomato and 1 egg yolk until blended together. Form into a very large, thin patty shape and grill or cook in a large, heavy-based frying pan on one side for 3 minutes, then on the other side for 2 minutes, until golden. Spread 1 warm naan with 2 tablespoons of Greek yogurt, scatter with the mint leaves and shredded lettuce, if using, and slip the large flattened kofta on top. Roll tightly and secure with cocktail sticks. Cut the kofta in half to serve 2.

sweet potato & raisin salad

Serves **6**
Preparation time **15 minutes**
Cooking time **25 minutes**

1 kg (2 lb) **sweet potatoes**
100 g (3½ oz) **raisins**
1 tablespoon **groundnut oil**
50 g (2 oz) **butter**
1 small **onion**, peeled and
   finely grated
½ teaspoon **ground ginger**
pinch of **saffron threads**
200 ml (7 fl oz) **water**
½ teaspoon **ground cinnamon**
1 tablespoon **sugar**
1 tablespoon **honey**
pinch of **salt** and **pepper**

Peel the sweet potatoes and cut into 2 cm (1 inch) thick rounds or pieces.

Soak the raisins in a bowl of very hot water for 5 minutes.

Heat the oil and butter in a large, heavy-based casserole and soften the onion over a gentle heat. Add the spices, salt and pepper and stir for 5 minutes. Moisten with the water. Once it bubbles, add the sweet potato and cook for 10 minutes.

Add the drained raisins, then the cinnamon, sugar and honey. Lower the heat and leave to simmer for 10 minutes, until the sauce is thick and rich.

Serve warm.

For spicy sweet potato salad, fry 2 chopped onions in 3 tablespoons of olive oil until golden. Add 1 teaspoon each of ground ginger, ground cumin and paprika, plus a pinch of salt, and stir for 5 minutes, then add the water and sweet potato as above. To serve, stir in the juice of 1 lemon, the chopped peel of a preserved lemon and 12 green olives. Drizzle with extra olive oil and garnish with finely chopped flat-leaf parsley.

orange & olive salad

Serves **6**
Preparation time **15 minutes**
Refrigeration **1 hour**

3 large **oranges**
3 **garlic cloves**, finely chopped
½ teaspoon **chilli powder**
2 tablespoons **olive oil**
2 tablespoons **lemon juice**
    (about 1 lemon)
150 g (5 oz) **Greek black
    olives**
salt

Peel the oranges, removing all pith and membrane. Cut the segments into pieces and put into a salad bowl.

Add the garlic to the bowl.

Season with the chilli powder, oil, lemon juice and salt to taste. Gently incorporate the olives.

Chill in the refrigerator for at least 1 hour. Serve cold.

For orange, olive & onion salad, prepare the oranges as above and scatter with the olives and a finely chopped mild red onion. Sprinkle over a dressing made with the juice of 1 lemon, 2 tablespoons of olive oil, ¼ teaspoon each of ground cumin and paprika, a pinch of chilli powder and salt to taste. Garnish with finely chopped flat-leaf parsley to serve.

garlic-fried chillies

Serves **6**
Preparation time **15 minutes**
Cooking time **5 minutes**

oil, for frying
6 **green chilli peppers**
2 **garlic cloves**, crushed
salt

Heat a little oil in a frying pan and fry the chillies, turning regularly. Transfer to a plate covered with kitchen paper, then arrange in a shallow dish.

Brown the garlic very rapidly in the frying pan.

Season the chillies with the garlic and salt to taste.

For garlic-roasted tomatoes, cut 12 ripe plum tomatoes in half lengthways and place cut side up in an ovenproof dish brushed with 2 tablespoons of olive oil. Tuck the unpeeled cloves from a whole head of garlic between the tomatoes. Sprinkle over 2 tablespoons of caster sugar, season with salt and black pepper to taste, and roast for 4 hours in a preheated oven, 140°C (275°F), Gas Mark 1.

tapenade

Serves **6**
Preparation time **15 minutes**

300 g (10 oz) **Greek black olives**
2 **garlic cloves**, crushed
1 tablespoon **thyme** or **marjoram**
2 tablespoons **olive oil**
pinch of **salt**

Pit the olives and place in a salad bowl.

Mix the garlic with the olives.

Add the herbs, oil and salt and mix well.

Serve well chilled.

For green olive tapenade, finely chop together 300 g (10 oz) pitted green olives, 1 tablespoon of capers and 50 g (2 oz) anchovy fillets. Stir in 2 tablespoons of olive oil, the juice of 1 lemon, 2 tablespoons of finely chopped flat-leaf parsley and 2 crushed garlic cloves. Mix well.

soups

harira fassia

Serves **6**
Preparation time **15 minutes**
Cooking time **40 minutes**

4 ripe **tomatoes**
1 tablespoon **tomato paste**
600 m! (1 pint) **water**
50 g (2 oz) **plain flour**
20 g (¾ oz) **butter**
2 **onions**, finely chopped
200 g (7 oz) **veal**, cubed
100 g (3½ oz) **lamb**, cubed
200 g (7 oz) **canned chickpeas**, drained
a few **celery leaves**
2 bunches of **coriander**, chopped
1 bunch of **flat-leaf parsley**, chopped
¼ teaspoon **pepper**
1 sachet of **saffron colorant**
pinch of **powdered saffron**
¼ teaspoon **ground ginger**
100 g (3½ oz) **green lentils**
50 g (2 oz) **short-grain rice**
salt

Peel the tomatoes and cut into very small pieces.

Blend the tomato paste with the half the water and the flour.

Place the butter in a large, heavy-based casserole with the tomatoes, onions, veal, lamb, chickpeas, celery leaves, half the coriander and all the parsley, spices and salt to taste. Cover with water and cook for 15 minutes, then add the lentils.

Leave to cook for a further 10 minutes until everything is cooked through, then add the remaining measured water. As soon as it returns to a boil, add the diluted tomato paste and stir with a spatula for 10 minutes to prevent lumps from forming.

Add the rice 15 minutes before the end.

Serve sprinkled with the remaining coriander.

For harira with pasta, omit the rice and add 75 g (3 oz) orzo (bird's-tongue pasta) or crushed vermicelli with the juice of 1 lemon 10 minutes before serving the soup. Garnish with lemon wedges and the remaining coriander and accompany with fresh dates.

couscous & aniseed soup

Serves **6**
Preparation time **2 minutes**
Cooking time **18 minutes**

1.5 litres (2½ pints) **water**
50 g (2 oz) **butter**
½ teaspoon **ground turmeric**
¼ teaspoon **pepper**
200 g (7 oz) **coarse-grain
   couscous**
1 tablespoon **ground aniseed**
salt

Put the water, butter, turmeric, pepper and salt to taste in a large saucepan. Bring to a boil, then tip in the couscous in a steady stream with half the aniseed.

Leave to simmer for 15 minutes over a low heat, stirring from time to time during cooking to prevent lumps from forming. If the couscous swells too much, add a little extra water.

Stir in the remaining aniseed and serve hot.

For chicken and couscous soup, fry a chopped onion in 2 tablespoons of olive oil until translucent. Add 500 g (1 lb) chicken breast, cut into strips, and cook, stirring, for 2 minutes. Add a medium sweet potato and a medium courgette, cut into cubes, the couscous, half the aniseed and the water. Simmer for 15 minutes over a low heat, as above. Stir in the remaining aniseed and serve hot, sprinkled with 1 tablespoon of chopped flat-leaf parsley.

harira

Serves **8–10**

Preparation time **about 25 minutes**, plus soaking

Cooking time **about 3 hours**

250 g (8 oz) **chickpeas**, soaked in cold water overnight

2 **chicken breasts**, halved

1.2 litres (2 pints) **chicken stock**

1.2 litres (2 pints) **water**

2 x 400 g (13 oz) cans **chopped tomatoes**

¼ teaspoon crumbled **saffron threads** (optional)

2 **onions**, chopped

125 g (4 oz) **long-grain rice**

50 g (2 oz) **green lentils**

2 tablespoons finely chopped **coriander**

2 tablespoons finely chopped **parsley**

salt and **pepper**

natural **yogurt** and **coriander** sprigs, to garnish

Drain the chickpeas, rinse under cold running water and drain again. Place them in a saucepan, cover with 5 cm (2 inches) of water and bring to the boil. Boil rapidly for 10 minutes, then lower the heat and simmer, partially covered, for up to 1¾ hours until tender, adding more water as necessary. Drain and set aside.

Place the chicken breasts, stock and water in a second saucepan. Bring to the boil, lower the heat, cover the pan and simmer for 10–15 minutes or until the chicken is just cooked. Remove the chicken from the stock, place it on a board and shred it, discarding the skin.

Set the shredded chicken aside. Add the chickpeas, tomatoes, saffron (if using), onions, rice and lentils to the stock remaining in the pan. Cover the pan and simmer for 30–35 minutes or until the rice and lentils are tender.

Add the shredded chicken, coriander and parsley just before serving. Heat the soup for a further 5 minutes without letting it boil. Season to taste and serve the soup, garnished with drizzles of natural yogurt and coriander sprigs.

For an economical harira, make up the soup as above, omitting the chicken breasts and saffron and adding ½ teaspoon of turmeric and ½ teaspoon of ground cinnamon instead.

quick chicken soup

Serves **6**
Preparation time **10 minutes**
Cooking time **30 minutes**

5 litres (8 pints) **water**
8 **chicken wings**
3 **tomatoes**
2 **potatoes**, peeled and halved
1 large **onion**, halved
1 tied bunch of **flat-leaf parsley**
1 tied bunch of **coriander**
¼ teaspoon **pepper**
¼ teaspoon **ground turmeric**
50 g (2 oz) **short-grain rice**
salt

Put the water in a large, heavy-based casserole with the chicken wings, tomatoes, potatoes, onion, herbs, pepper, turmeric and salt to taste and bring to a boil. Cook for 25 minutes.

Remove the herbs. Remove and reserve the chicken wings.

Strain the vegetables, reserving the stock, and pass them through a food mill or blender until smooth.

Return the blended vegetables, the stock and the chicken wings to the pot and return to the boil. Add the rice in a steady stream, stir, and cook for a further 5 minutes.

For chicken soup with rice, fry 750 g (1 ½ lb) sliced carrots in 25 g (1 oz) butter over medium heat for 15 minutes. Add 1.2 litres (2 pints) chicken stock and 250 ml (8 fl oz) milk, bring to the boil, then simmer for 10 minutes, or until the carrots are tender. Process briefly to form a rough consistency, then add 150 g (5 oz) cooked rice and ½ tablespoon of crushed toasted cumin seeds. Heat through, then remove from the heat. Whisk in 2 egg yolks, then stir in 125 g (4 oz) shredded cooked chicken breast and 2 tablespoons of chopped mint.

lamb & vegetable chorba

Serves **6**
Preparation time **20 minutes**
Cooking time **35 minutes**

1 litre (1¾ pints) **water**
200 g (7 oz) **lamb**, cubed
1 **onion**, sliced in fine strips
¼ teaspoon **pepper**
½ teaspoon **ground turmeric**
4 **carrots**, trimmed and cubed
2 **leeks**, trimmed and cubed
3 **potatoes**, cubed
3 **turnips**, trimmed and cubed
2 **tomatoes**, cubed
1 bunch of **coriander**, snipped
1 bunch of **flat-leaf parsley**,
   snipped
50 g (2 oz) **vermicelli**
1 tablespoon **tomato paste**
20 g (¾ oz) **butter**
salt

Bring the water to the boil in a large saucepan, then add the meat, onion, pepper, turmeric and salt to taste. Leave to cook for 20 minutes.

Add all the prepared vegetables. Add the snipped coriander and parsley to the pan.

Leave to simmer for a further 12 minutes until the vegetables are cooked, then add the vermicelli and tomato paste and continue to cook for 8 minutes.

Stir in the butter just before serving.

For fish & vegetable chorba, omit the lamb. Make the recipe as above, adding 500 g (1 lb) firm white fish fillets, cut into chunks, with the vermicelli and tomato paste. Drizzle over 2 tablespoons of harissa to serve.

tagines

chicken with parsley

Serves **6**
Preparation time **15 minutes**
Cooking time **25 minutes**

3 tablespoons **olive oil**
1 large **onion**, finely chopped
3 **garlic cloves**, finely chopped
1 whole **chicken**, weighing
    about 1.5 kg (3 lb), cut into
    pieces
pinch of **saffron**
250 ml (8 fl oz) **water**
2 large **tomatoes**
1 bunch of **flat-leaf parsley**,
    snipped
1 **preserved lemon**, cut into
    fine strips
300 g (10 oz) **green olives**,
    pitted and rinsed
¼ teaspoon **pepper**
salt

Heat the oil in a large, heavy-based casserole and soften the onion and garlic.

Season the chicken pieces and add to the pot, one at a time, and allow to brown on all sides for 5 minutes. Add the saffron and the water, cover the pot, and leave to cook over a medium heat for 15 minutes.

Skin the tomatoes and cut into small pieces. Add to the pot with the parsley and lemon, then lower the heat a little, and let the sauce reduce slightly. Add the olives and season with the pepper and salt, to taste.

Serve the chicken with the sauce and olives spooned around the sides.

For chicken with artichoke hearts, thaw 500 g (1 lb) frozen artichoke hearts, cut them into quarters and add to the pot when the chicken has been cooking for 10 minutes, with a little extra water if necessary. Instead of using a whole bunch of parsley, use half parsley and half coriander.

chicken with carrots

Serves **6**

Preparation time **20 minutes**

Cooking time **30 minutes**

1 whole **chicken**, weighing
about 1.5 kg (3 lb), cut
into pieces

2 tablespoons **olive oil**

1 large **onion**, finely chopped

2 large **garlic cloves**, crushed

pinch of **saffron**

¼ teaspoon **ground turmeric**

¼ teaspoon **ground ginger**

250 ml (8 fl oz) **water**

1 kg (2 lb) **carrots**, trimmed
and cut into sticks

1 tablespoon chopped **flat-leaf
parsley**

1 **lemon**, juiced

pinch of **pepper**

salt

Season the chicken.

Heat the oil in a large, heavy-based casserole and
brown the chicken pieces with the onion, garlic and
spices.

Add the water and simmer over a medium heat for
10 minutes, then add the carrots and cook for a further
15 minutes.

Sprinkle with the parsley and the lemon juice when
the sauce has reduced slightly.

Remove from the heat after 5 minutes and season
with a pinch of pepper and salt to taste.

For chicken with chestnuts, gently fry 1 sliced onion in
2 tablespoons of olive oil until soft and starting to brown.
Stir in ½ teaspoon each of ground cinnamon and ginger
and a pinch of saffron, then add the chicken pieces and
brown them all over. Add 250 ml (8 fl oz) water and
simmer over a medium heat for 25–30 minutes, until
the chicken is tender. Remove the chicken pieces, then
reduce the sauce. Stir in 1 tablespoon of honey, season
to taste, then add 400 g (13 oz) vacuum-packed roasted
whole chestnuts. Return the chicken to the pan, adding
a little water if necessary, and simmer for 4–5 minutes
to heat through.

moroccan chicken & harissa

Serves **4**
Preparation time **20 minutes**
Cooking time **35 minutes**

1 **onion**, very finely chopped
2 teaspoons **paprika**
1 teaspoon **cumin seeds**
4 x 125 g (4 oz) boneless,
  skinless **chicken breasts**
1 bunch of **coriander**, finely
  chopped
4 tablespoons **lemon juice**
3 tablespoons **olive oil**
salt and **pepper**

Harissa
4 **red peppers**
4 large **red chillies**
2 **garlic cloves**, crushed
½ teaspoon **coriander seeds**
1 teaspoon **caraway seeds**
5 tablespoons **olive oil**

Make the harissa by heating a griddle pan (or frying pan). Add the whole red peppers and cook for 15 minutes, turning occasionally. The skins will blacken and start to lift. Place the peppers in a plastic bag, seal the bag and set aside (this encourages them to 'sweat', making it easier to remove their skins). When cool enough to handle, remove the skin, cores and seeds and place the flesh in a blender or food processor.

Remove the skin, cores and seeds from the chillies in the same way and add the flesh to the blender with the garlic, coriander and caraway seeds and olive oil. Process to a smooth paste. If not required immediately, place the harissa in a sealable container and pour a thin layer of olive oil over the top. Cover with a lid and refrigerate.

Clean the griddle pan (or frying pan) and reheat it. Place the onion in a bowl, add the paprika and cumin seeds and mix together. Rub the onion and spice mixture into the chicken breasts. Cook the chicken for 10 minutes on each side, turning once. Remove from the pan.

Place the coriander in a bowl and add the lemon juice, olive oil and a little seasoning. Add the chicken to the bowl and toss well. Serve with rice and the harissa.

For spinach salad, to serve as an accompaniment, rinse and tear 400 g (13 oz) spinach and add to a pan with any residual water. Cover and cook for 1–2 minutes until wilted. Stir in 1 clove chopped garlic, 100 g (3½ oz) Greek yogurt, salt and pepper. Warm and serve.

chicken 'mchermel'

Serves **6**
Preparation time **10 minutes**
Cooking time **25 minutes**

4 tablespoons **olive oil**
3 **onions**, finely chopped
1 whole **chicken**, weighing
    about 1.5 kg (3 lb), cut
    into pieces
¼ teaspoon **ground turmeric**
pinch of **saffron**
¼ teaspoon **ground ginger**
400 ml (14 fl oz) **water**
4 **coriander stalks**, snipped
4 **parsley stalks**, snipped
¼ teaspoon **ground cumin**
½ teaspoon **sweet paprika**
300 g (10 oz) **green olives**,
    pitted and rinsed
1 **lemon**, juiced
2 **preserved lemons**,
    to garnish
pinch of **pepper**
salt

Heat the olive oil in a large, heavy-based ovenproof dish and brown the onions for 3 minutes.

Add the chicken pieces to the pan and season with the turmeric, saffron, ginger, pepper and salt to taste. Stir in 300 ml (10 fl oz) of the water, cover the pan, and leave to simmer over a low heat for around 10 minutes.

Stir in the remaining water, the herbs, cumin and paprika. Allow to reduce for around 10 minutes until the sauce has thickened. Add the olives and the lemon juice, and simmer for a further 5 minutes.

Meanwhile, rinse the preserved lemons, cut them in half, and remove the pulp. Cut the rind into strips.

Transfer the chicken to a serving platter, pour the sauce around it, and garnish with the strips of preserved lemon.

For baked chicken with lemons, mix ½ teaspoon each of ground cinnamon and turmeric, plus seasoning to taste, and rub evenly over the chicken. Fry on all sides in 2 tablespoons of olive oil, then transfer to a lidded ovenproof dish. Fry a sliced large onion until soft, then stir in 2 teaspoons of grated fresh root ginger and 600 ml (1 pint) hot chicken stock. Pour over the chicken. Cover and cook in a preheated oven, 190°C (375°F), Gas Mark 5, for 30 minutes. Add 2 preserved lemons cut into wedges, 75 g (3 oz) olives and 1 tablespoon of honey. Bake, uncovered, for a further 45 minutes, until tender. Stir in 4 tablespoons of chopped coriander to serve.

spicy stuffed chicken

Serves **6**
Preparation time **10 minutes**
Cooking time **1 hour 5 minutes**

3 **garlic cloves**, finely chopped
1 small **red chilli pepper**,
  sliced in thin rings
4 tablespoons **olive oil**
1 **lemon**, juiced
1 tablespoon **honey**
3 tablespoons **tomato juice**
1 tablespoon **ground cumin**
1 tablespoon **crushed Nora
  peppercorns**
1 tablespoon **ground ginger**
1 whole **chicken**, weighing
  about 1.5 kg (3 lb)
2 **bay leaves**
salt and **pepper**

Stuffing
250 g (8 oz) **raisins**
1 **garlic clove**, roughly chopped
1 **onion**, roughly chopped
25 g (1 oz) **butter**
½ teaspoon **ground cinnamon**
½ teaspoon **ground cumin**
2 tablespoons **blanched
  almonds**
salt and **pepper**

Mix together the garlic, chilli, oil, lemon juice, honey, tomato juice and all the spices and stir well. Season to taste and set aside.

Make the stuffing by soaking the raisins in a little warm water. Purée the garlic and onion together in a blender. Melt the butter in a small pan and quickly brown the garlic and onion. Stir in the cinnamon and cumin and cook for around 2 minutes. Add the drained raisins and the almonds. Season and cook for a further 2 minutes. Set aside to cool.

Preheat the oven to 220°C (425°F), Gas Mark 6.

Fill the cavity of the chicken with the stuffing. Place in an ovenproof dish and brush with the sauce. Place the bay leaves on top. Roast for around 1 hour, basting from time to time with the cooking juices. Cut the chicken into pieces and serve hot with the stuffing and sauce.

For chicken with couscous stuffing, soak 75 g (3 oz) chopped dried apricots in a little hot water. Prepare 250 g (8 oz) instant couscous according to the packet instructions, adding 50 g (2 oz) butter to the boiling water. Gently fry 2 chopped onions in 25 g (1 oz) butter until soft, then stir in 2 teaspoons of cinnamon and cook for a further 2 minutes. Add the onions to the couscous with the apricots and 3 tablespoons of the soaking water, 2 tablespoons of sliced blanched almonds and 1 tablespoon of honey. Season to taste, then fill the cavity of the chicken with the stuffing and cook as above.

roast chicken with chermoula

Serves **6**

Preparation time **20 minutes**, plus marinating

Cooking time **45 minutes**

3 **garlic cloves**
1 bunch of **coriander**
1 **lemon**, juiced
½ teaspoon **ground cumin**
¾ teaspoon **paprika**
pinch of **cayenne pepper**
3 tablespoons **sunflower oil**
½ teaspoon **salt**
3 small **chickens**, cut in two

Make the chermoula marinade by chopping the garlic and coriander together. Mix in a bowl with the lemon juice, spices, oil and salt.

Coat the chicken with half the marinade and refrigerate for 1 hour.

Preheat the oven to 220°C (425°F), Gas Mark 7.

Transfer the chicken to an ovenproof dish, drizzle over the remaining marinade, and cook for around 45 minutes.

For spring vegetables to serve as an accompaniment, bring 750 ml (1¼ pints) chicken stock to the boil, then add 250 g (8 oz) each of baby carrots and broad beans and 6 sliced spring onions. Cook for 8–10 minutes, until the carrots and broad beans are almost tender. Add 250 g (8 oz) fresh young peas and cook for a further 2 minutes. Stir in 2 tablespoons each of chopped coriander and flat-leaf parsley and 1 tablespoon of chopped mint and season to taste.

chicken k'dra

Serves **4**
Preparation time **15 minutes**
Cooking time **2 hours
5 minutes**

2 tablespoons **olive oil**
8 boneless, skinless **chicken
thighs**, cut into large chunks
2 **onions**, thinly sliced
2 **garlic cloves**, finely chopped
2 tablespoons **plain flour**
900 ml (1½ pints) **chicken
stock**
grated rind and juice of
1 **lemon**
2 large pinches **saffron
threads**
1 **cinnamon stick**, halved
2 x 410 g (13½ oz) cans
chickpeas, drained
500 g (1 lb) **potatoes**, cut into
chunks
salt and **pepper**
parsley or **mixed parsley
and mint**, chopped, to
garnish

Heat the oil in a large frying pan, add the chicken and onions and fry, in batches if necessary, for 5 minutes until golden.

Stir in the garlic, then mix in the flour. Add the stock, lemon rind and juice, saffron, cinnamon and plenty of seasoning and bring to the boil.

Preheat the oven to 180°C (350°F), Gas Mark 4.

Transfer to a tagine or casserole dish. Add the chickpeas and potatoes, mix together, then cover and cook for 2 hours.

Stir, then sprinkle with the herbs. Spoon into shallow bowls and serve with warm pitta breads.

For saffron chicken with mixed vegetables, reduce the stock to 600 ml (1 pint) and add a 400 g (13 oz) can of chopped tomatoes. Add 1 can of chickpeas only, then mix in 125 g (4 oz) thickly sliced okra and 125 g (4 oz) thickly sliced green beans 10 minutes before the end of cooking.

speedy spiced chicken tagine

Serves **4**
Preparation time **20 minutes**
Cooking time **55 minutes**

1 tablespoon **olive oil**
8 **chicken thighs**, skinned
1 **onion**, sliced
2 **garlic cloves**, finely chopped
500 g (1 lb) **plum tomatoes**,
   skinned (optional), cut into
   chunks
1 teaspoon **ground turmeric**
1 **cinnamon stick**, halved
2.5 cm (1 inch) piece **fresh
   ginger**, grated
2 teaspoons **runny honey**
100 g (3½ oz) ready-to-eat
   dried apricots, quartered
200 g (7 oz) **couscous**
450 ml (¾ pint) boiling **water**
grated rind and juice of
   1 **lemon**
small bunch of **coriander**,
   roughly chopped
salt and **pepper**

Heat the oil in a large frying pan, add the chicken and fry until browned on both sides. Lift out and transfer to a tagine or casserole dish. Add the onion to the pan and fry until golden.

Stir in the garlic, tomatoes, spices and honey. Add the apricots and a little salt and pepper and heat through. Spoon over the chicken, cover the dish and bake in a preheated oven, 180°C (350°F), Gas Mark 4, for 45 minutes or until the chicken is cooked through.

When the chicken is almost ready, soak the couscous in boiling water for 5 minutes. Stir in the lemon rind and juice, coriander and seasoning. Spoon onto plates and top with the chicken and tomatoes, discarding the cinnamon stick just before eating.

For chicken & vegetable tagine, use just 4 chicken thigh joints and add 1 diced carrot, 1 cored, deseeded and diced red pepper and 150 g (5 oz) frozen broad beans. Replace the cinnamon with 2 teaspoons harissa paste and add 150 ml (¼ pint) chicken stock. Cook as above, adding 100 g (3½ oz) thickly sliced okra or green beans for the last 15 minutes of cooking. Sprinkle with chopped coriander or mint and serve with rice.

quail with raisins

Serves **6**
Preparation time **10 minutes**
Cooking time **30 minutes**

2 tablespoons **sunflower oil**
65 g (2½ oz) **butter**
3 large **onions**, finely chopped
12 small **quail**
1 **cinnamon stick**
¼ teaspoon **ground ginger**
pinch of **saffron**
150 ml (¼ pint) **water**
300 g (10 oz) **raisins**
½ teaspoon **ground cinnamon**
2 tablespoons **sugar**
2 tablespoons **honey**
¼ teaspoon **pepper**
½ teaspoon **salt**

Heat the oil and half the butter in a large, heavy-based casserole and soften the onions.

Add the quail, cinnamon stick, ginger, saffron and water and cook for 20 minutes.

Stir in the remaining butter, the raisins, ground cinnamon, sugar, honey, pepper and salt. Simmer until the sauce has reduced and has a good caramel colour.

For spiced vegetables to serve as an accompaniment, fry 2 onions, cut into wedges, and 2 crushed garlic cloves in 4 tablespoons of olive oil until soft. Add 4 carrots, cut into large batons, and 2 fennel bulbs, cut into wedges, and cook for about 3 minutes until softened, then add 2 sliced courgettes and cook for a further 2 minutes. Add 2 teaspoons of turmeric, 1 teaspoon of ground cumin and ½ teaspoon of ground ginger and cook, stirring, for 1 minute. Stir in 2 large, ripe, peeled and diced tomatoes and season to taste with salt and black pepper. Cover and cook over a low heat, stirring occasionally, for about 10 minutes, or until the vegetables are just tender.

meatballs in tomato sauce

Serves **6**
Preparation time **15 minutes**
Cooking time **15 minutes**

1 **onion**, finely chopped
1 bunch of **flat-leaf parsley**,
   snipped
500 g (1 lb) **minced beef or
   lamb** (15% fat content)
1 tablespoon **paprika**
½ teaspoon **ground cumin**
3 tablespoons **groundnut oil**
300 ml (10 fl oz) **passata**
   (sieved tomatoes)
¼ teaspoon **tomato paste**
250 ml (8 fl oz) **water**
6 **eggs**
salt and **pepper**

Place the onion and parsley in a large bowl with the meat, salt to taste, and half the paprika and cumin. Mix well and form into balls the size of a walnut. Set aside.

Pour the oil into a tagine and add the passata, salt and pepper to taste, and the remaining spices. Cook for 2 minutes, then add the tomato paste and water and cook until the sauce bubbles.

Place the meatballs carefully in the tagine and stir until they are sealed on all sides. Break the eggs over the meatballs and leave to bubble gently over a very low heat until the eggs are cooked.

Serve once the sauce has reduced.

For meatballs in spicy sun-dried tomato sauce, first rehydrate 50 g (2 oz) sun-dried tomatoes in boiling water, then process them until smooth. Prepare the meatballs as above and set aside. Add the oil, passata and seasoning to the tagine with 3 crushed garlic cloves and a finely chopped red chilli, the remaining paprika and cumin and 1 teaspoon each of ground coriander and cinnamon. Cook for 2 minutes, then add the puréed sun-dried tomatoes, 250 ml (8 fl oz) well-flavoured stock and 2 tablespoons of chopped coriander. Cook until the sauce bubbles, then complete the recipe as above.

moroccan lamb

Serves **2**
Preparation time **15 minutes**,
 plus marinating
Cooking time **1½ hours**

1 teaspoon **ground ginger**
1 teaspoon **ground cumin**
1 teaspoon **ground paprika**
1 **cinnamon stick**
50 ml (2 fl oz) **orange juice**
250 g (8 oz) lean **lamb**, cut
 into 5 cm (2 inch) cubes
125 g (4 oz) **button onions or
 shallots**, unpeeled
1 tablespoon **olive oil**
1 **garlic clove**, crushed
2 teaspoons **plain flour**
2 teaspoons **tomato purée**
125 ml (4 fl oz) **lamb stock**
3 tablespoons **sherry**
50 g (2 oz) ready-to-eat **dried
 apricots**
300 g (10 oz) canned
 chickpeas, rinsed and
 drained
salt and **pepper**
sprigs of **coriander** or **flat-leaf
 parsley**, to garnish

Put the spices in a large bowl and pour the orange juice over them. Add the lamb and mix well, then cover and leave in a cool place for at least 1 hour, or preferably overnight, in the refrigerator.

Put the onions or shallots in a heatproof bowl and cover with boiling water. Leave for 2 minutes. Drain and refresh under cold water, then peel.

Heat the oil in a large, flameproof casserole. Remove the lamb from the marinade and pat dry with kitchen paper. Brown over a high heat until golden all over. Using a slotted spoon, remove the lamb and set aside. Reduce the heat slightly and, adding a little more oil if necessary, cook the onions or shallots and garlic for 3 minutes or until just beginning to brown. Return the meat to the pan and stir in the flour and tomato purée. Cook for 1 minute.

Add the marinade to the pan with the stock, sherry and seasoning. Bring to the boil, then reduce the heat, cover and place in a preheated oven, 180°C (350°F), Gas Mark 4, for 1 hour. Add the apricots and chickpeas and cook for a further 15 minutes. Serve with couscous cooked according to the packet instructions and garnished with sprigs of coriander or flat-leaf parsley.

For moroccan chicken, replace the lamb with the same quantity of chicken breast meat, cut into cubes, and cook as above. Replace the apricots with the same quantity of raisins.

lamb with orange & chickpeas

Serves **8**

Preparation time **25 minutes**,
plus overnight soaking

Cooking time **2½ hours**

225 g (7½ oz) **chickpeas**,
soaked in cold water
overnight

4 tablespoons **olive oil**

2 teaspoons **ground cumin**

1 teaspoon each **ground
cinnamon, ground ginger,
ground turmeric**

½ teaspoon **saffron threads**

1.5 kg (3 lb) **shoulder of
lamb**, trimmed of all fat and
cut into 2.5 cm (1 inch) cubes

2 **onions**, roughly chopped

3 **garlic cloves**, finely chopped

2 **tomatoes**, skinned,
deseeded and chopped

12 pitted **black olives**, sliced

grated rind of 1 **unwaxed
lemon**

grated rind of 1 **unwaxed
orange**

6 tablespoons chopped
coriander

salt and **pepper**

Drain and rinse the chickpeas. Place them in a large saucepan and cover with water. Bring to the boil, then cover and simmer for about 1–1½ hours, until tender.

Meanwhile, combine half the olive oil with the cumin, cinnamon, ginger, turmeric and saffron in a large bowl, plus ½ teaspoon each salt and pepper. Add the cubed lamb, toss and set aside in a cool place for 20 minutes. Wipe out the pan, heat the remaining oil and fry the lamb in batches until well browned; transfer to a plate to drain.

Add the onions to the pan and cook, stirring constantly, until browned. Add the garlic, tomatoes and 250 ml (8 fl oz) water, stirring and scraping the base of the pan. Return the lamb to the pan and add water to just cover. Bring to the boil, skim off any surface foam, then cover and simmer for about 1 hour or until the meat is tender.

Drain the chickpeas, reserving the cooking liquid. Add the chickpeas and about 250 ml (8 fl oz) of the cooking liquid to the lamb. Simmer for 30 minutes. Stir in the olives and lemon and orange rind and simmer for 30 minutes. Stir in half the coriander, using the remainder to garnish.

For easy lamb tagine, place 1.5 kg (3 lb) cubed shoulder of lamb in a pan with 1 teaspoon of salt, cover with water and bring slowly to the boil. Skim and add a pinch of saffron, 1 whole, unpeeled onion and 1½ teaspoons each of crushed coriander seeds and black peppercorns. Simmer for 2 hours, then discard the onion. Cool the stock and skim the fat, then add ½ teaspoon of turmeric and the juice of 2 small oranges and reheat gently.

lamb & prune tagine with barley

Serves **4**
Preparation time **15 minutes**
Cooking time **1–1¼ hours**

olive oil spray

625 g (1¼ lb) lean diced **lamb**

1 **red onion**, chopped

1 **carrot**, peeled and chopped

1 teaspoon **paprika**

1 teaspoon **ground coriander**

1 teaspoon **fennel seeds**

3 cm (1¼ inch) **cinnamon stick**

2 **garlic cloves**, crushed

2 **bay leaves**

2 tablespoons **lime juice**

750 ml (1¼ pints) **chicken stock**

75 g (3 oz) **dried prunes**

400 g (13 oz) can chopped **tomatoes**

65 g (2½ oz) **pearl barley**

15 g (½ oz) chopped **coriander**, plus extra sprigs to garnish

1 tablespoon **lime juice**, to garnish

400 g (13 oz) **couscous**

salt and **pepper**

Heat a large saucepan or 2 litre (3½ pint) flameproof casserole dish, spray lightly with oil and cook the lamb briefly, in batches if necessary, until brown. Remove the lamb with a slotted spoon, add the onion and carrot to the pan and cook briefly to brown. Return the lamb, stir in all the remaining ingredients and season to taste.

Simmer covered for 1 hour or until the lamb is tender. At the end of the cooking time, stir in the coriander and lime juice.

Meanwhile, cook the couscous according to the instructions on the packet and set aside for 5 minutes.

Serve the hot tagine over the couscous and garnish with coriander sprigs.

For pork & apricot tagine, replace the lamb with the same quantity of diced pork and replace the dried prunes with dried apricots. Toast a generous handful of split almonds in a dry pan over a medium heat, then stir into the casserole along with the other ingredients.

lamb with quince

Serves **6**
Preparation time **20 minutes**
Cooking time **30 minutes**

1.25 kg (2½ lb) **leg or
  shoulder of lamb**, cubed
2 **onions**, finely chopped
250 ml (8 fl oz) **water**
2 tablespoons **groundnut oil**
50 g (2 oz) **butter**
1 **cinnamon stick**
pinch of **saffron**
½ teaspoon **ground ginger**
1 kg (2 lb) **quince**
½ teaspoon **ground cinnamon**
2 tablespoons **sugar**
2 tablespoons **honey**
pinch of **pepper**
salt

Place the lamb and onions in a large, heavy-based casserole with the water, oil, half the butter, the cinnamon stick, saffron and ginger. Season, then cover the dish and cook over a medium heat for 20 minutes.

Meanwhile, peel and core the quince and cut into eighths. Put the remaining butter, the ground cinnamon, sugar and honey in a saucepan and moisten with 2 ladlefuls of the cooking juices from the casserole.

Tip in the quince and cook until they are caramelized.

Transfer the meat to a round serving plate and serve with the sauce and the quince.

For lamb with quince & caramelized shallots,
use only 1 chopped onion when cooking the meat. Blanch 500 g (1 lb) shallots in boiling water for 5 minutes. When cool enough to handle, peel and trim the shallots and fry them in 2 tablespoons of groundnut oil for 5–10 minutes, until starting to colour. Caramelize with the quince, adding more of the meat cooking juices if necessary.

moroccan meatball tagine

Serves **4**
Preparation time **15 minutes**
Cooking time **40 minutes**

2 small **onions**, finely chopped
2 tablespoons **raisins**
750 g (1 ½ lb) **minced beef**
1 tablespoon **tomato purée**
3 teaspoons **curry powder**
3 tablespoons **olive oil**
½ teaspoon **ground cinnamon**
625 g (1 ¼ lb) can chopped
   tomatoes
½ **lemon**, juiced
2 **celery sticks**, thickly sliced
1 large or 2 medium
   courgettes, roughly chopped
175 g (6 oz) **frozen peas**

Mix together half the onions, the raisins, minced beef, tomato purée and curry powder in a bowl. Using your hands, knead to combine the mixture evenly. Form the mixture into 24 meatballs.

Heat 1 tablespoon of the oil in a saucepan, add the meatballs, in small batches, and cook until browned all over. Tip out the excess fat and put all the meatballs in the pan. Add the cinnamon, tomatoes and lemon juice, cover and simmer gently for 25 minutes until the meatballs are cooked.

Meanwhile, heat the remaining oil in a large frying pan, add the celery and courgettes and cook until soft and starting to brown. Add the peas and cook for a further 5 minutes until the peas are tender.

Stir the courgette mixture into the meatball mixture just before serving.

For coriander & apricot couscous to serve as an accompaniment, put 200 g (7 oz) instant couscous in a large, heatproof bowl with 50 g (2 oz) chopped ready-to-eat dried apricots. Pour over boiling hot vegetable stock to just cover the couscous. Cover and leave to stand for 10–12 minutes until all the water has been absorbed. Meanwhile, chop 2 large, ripe tomatoes and finely chop 2 tablespoons coriander leaves. Fluff up the couscous with a fork and tip into a warmed serving dish. Stir in the tomatoes, coriander and 2 tablespoons of olive oil; season to taste. Toss well to mix and serve with the tagine.

lamb with apricots

Serves **6**
Preparation time **20 minutes**
Cooking time **1¼ hours**

1 **orange**
150 g (5 oz) **dried apricots**
2 tablespoons **olive oil**
1 large **onion**, finely sliced
1.25 kg (2½ lb) **shoulder of lamb**, cubed
½ teaspoon **ground cumin**
¼ teaspoon **ground cinnamon**
1 tablespoon **ground almonds**
300 ml (½ pint) **water**
1 tablespoon **white sesame seeds**
½ bunch of **coriander**, snipped (optional)
salt and **pepper**

Wash the orange, then zest the rind. Squeeze the juice and soak the apricots in the juice to swell.

Heat the oil in a large, heavy-based casserole and brown the onion for around 10 minutes, stirring from time to time.

Add the meat, cumin, cinnamon and salt and pepper to taste and stir well for 5 minutes. Pour in the orange juice with the apricots, orange rind, almonds and water. Cover, and bring to a simmer over a medium heat. When the juice is bubbling, lower the heat and continue to cook, stirring from time to time, for about 40 minutes, or until the lamb is cooked.

Meanwhile, dry-toast the sesame seeds in a frying pan. They should become golden but not blackened.

Transfer the cooked lamb to a serving platter and sprinkle with the sesame seeds and coriander, if using.

For courgette purée to serve as an accompaniment, thickly slice 500 g (1 lb) courgettes and steam until tender. Drain, chop and mash them well in a colander to release the juices. Heat 2 tablespoons of olive oil in a large frying pan and soften 500 g (1 lb) small plum tomatoes with 6 sliced garlic cloves over medium heat. When the garlic begins to colour, add the courgette purée, season to taste with salt and black pepper, and stir in 2 tablespoons of chopped coriander. Serve drizzled with olive oil.

lamb with mushrooms

Serves **6**
Preparation time **15 minutes**
Cooking time **25 minutes**

4 tablespoons **olive oil**
1.25 kg (2½ lb) l**eg or
   shoulder of lamb**, cubed
1 **onion**, finely chopped
2 **garlic cloves**, finely chopped
350 ml (12 fl oz) **water**
½ teaspoon **ground ginger**
pinch of **saffron**
50 g (1½ lb) **chestnut
   mushrooms**, peeled and
   sliced
80 g jar of **porcini mushrooms
   in white truffle paste** or
   1 x 850 ml (28 fl oz) can of
   white truffles (optional)
½ bunch of **flat-leaf parsley**,
   snipped
½ bunch of **coriander**, snipped
salt and **pepper**
chopped **coriander** or **flat-leaf
   parsley**, to garnish

Heat the olive oil in a large, heavy-based casserole and
cook the meat, onion and garlic together for 2 minutes.

Add the water, ginger, saffron and salt and pepper to
taste. Cover and cook for 15 minutes.

Stir in the chestnut mushrooms (along with the porcini
mushrooms in white truffle paste or white truffles, if
using), and the parsley and coriander. Allow to simmer
for a further 5–7 minutes over a low heat until the sauce
has reduced.

Transfer to a serving platter, with the meat arranged
around the truffles and garnished with chopped
coriander or flat-leaf parsley.

For pomegranate lamb, heat 4 tablespoons of olive
oil and briefly fry 3 crushed cardamom seeds,
3 cloves and 1 teaspoon of fenugreek seeds. Remove
the spices, then add 1.25 kg (2½ lb) cubed lamb,
1 finely chopped onion, 2 finely chopped garlic cloves
and ½ teaspoon of ground ginger. Cook for 2 minutes to
brown the meat, then gradually stir in 350 ml (12 fl oz)
pomegranate juice. Add ½ teaspoon each of ground
cumin, cinnamon and mace, season with salt and
pepper to taste and cook for a further 1 minute. Stir in
6 tablespoons of plain yogurt, then cover and cook over
a very low heat for about 30 minutes, or until the meat is
tender, stirring occasionally and adding a little water
if necessary.

'mderbel' tagine with aubergine

Serves **6**
Preparation time **15 minutes**
Cooking time **40 minutes**

oil, for frying
2 medium **aubergines**,
   trimmed and thickly sliced
½ teaspoon **paprika**
½ teaspoon **ground cumin**
4 **garlic cloves**, 1 crushed,
   3 finely chopped
½ **lemon**, juiced
3 tablespoons **olive oil**
1 large **onion**, finely chopped
½ teaspoon **ground turmeric**
pinch of **saffron**
½ teaspoon **ground ginger**
¼ teaspoon **pepper**
1.25 kg (2½ lb) **shoulder**
   of lamb, cubed
300 ml (½ pint) **water**
salt

Heat the oil and fry the aubergines on both sides, then remove and drain. Cut them roughly into smaller pieces, then brown in a frying pan with the paprika, cumin, the crushed garlic clove and a little salt.

Remove from the heat and add the lemon juice.

Heat the olive oil in a heavy-based casserole and brown the onion and chopped garlic, and the remaining spices. Add the meat, then pour in the water. Cover and leave to simmer for around 30 minutes. Remove the lid and reduce the sauce until thick.

Arrange the meat on a plate and serve the aubergine mixture on top.

For warm potato salad to serve as an accompaniment, steam 1 kg (2 lb) small new potatoes until tender. Toss in a dressing of 6 tablespoons of olive oil, the juice of 1 lemon, 1 teaspoon each of ground cumin and paprika and salt to taste. Stir in a finely chopped red onion and 4 tablespoons of chopped flat-leaf parsley.

chicken, lemon & olive tagine

Serves **4**
Preparation time **20 minutes**
Cooking time **1 hour**

1.5 kg (3 lb) **chicken**
about 4 tablespoons **olive oil**
12 **baby onions**, peeled but
   left whole
2 **garlic cloves**, crushed
1 teaspoon each **ground**
   cumin, **ground ginger**,
   ground turmeric
½ teaspoon **ground cinnamon**
450 ml (¾ pint) **chicken stock**
125 g (4 oz) **kalamata olives**
1 **preserved lemon**, pulp and
   skin discarded, chopped
2 tablespoons chopped
   coriander
salt and **pepper**

Joint the chicken into 8 pieces (or ask your butcher to do this for you). Heat the oil in a flameproof casserole and brown the chicken on all sides. Remove the pieces with a slotted spoon and set aside.

Add the onions, garlic and spices and sauté over a low heat for 10 minutes until just golden. Return the chicken to the pan, stir in the stock and bring to the boil. Cover and simmer gently for 30 minutes.

Stir in the olives, preserved lemon and coriander and cook for a further 15–20 minutes until the chicken is really tender. Taste and adjust the seasoning, if necessary.

For sweet spinach to serve as an accompaniment, steam 500 g (1 lb) rinsed and drained young spinach leaves until just wilted. Drain thoroughly, then roughly chop the spinach and drain again. Heat 2 tablespoons of olive oil in a pan and gently fry 1 finely chopped red onion for 2 minutes, or until translucent. Add 3 crushed garlic cloves, ¼ teaspoon of chilli flakes, 50 g (2 oz) pine nuts, 50 g (2 oz) raisins and 1 teaspoon of soft brown sugar. Stir in the chopped spinach and cook for a further 2 minutes, until warmed through.

rabbit in spicy sauce

Serves **6**
Preparation time **15 minutes**
Cooking time **25 minutes**

1 prepared **rabbit**, cut into
   8 pieces
3 tablespoons **olive oil**
1 large **onion**, chopped
3 **garlic cloves**, crushed
1 tablespoon **paprika**
½ teaspoon **ground cumin**
pinch of **cayenne pepper**
¼ teaspoon **pepper**
300 ml (10 fl oz) **water**
2 tablespoons **white wine**
   vinegar
coarse salt

Rub the rabbit pieces with the salt. Soak in water for several minutes.

Heat the oil in a casserole and soften the onion and garlic for 2 minutes. Add the drained rabbit and the spices.

Pour in the water and simmer over a low heat for 20 minutes to reduce the sauce.

Remove from the heat and stir in the vinegar.

For rabbit tagine with prunes, follow the recipe as above, replacing the paprika, cumin and cayenne with ½ teaspoon each of ground ginger and cinnamon. Add 75 g (3 oz) chopped ready-to-eat dried prunes and 1 tablespoon of honey to the sauce 5 minutes before the end of cooking time, and stir in the juice of 1 lemon instead of the vinegar.

chickpea tagine

Serves **4**
Preparation time **15 minutes**
Cooking time **40 minutes**

100 ml (3½ fl oz) **extra-virgin olive oil**
1 large **onion**, finely chopped
2 **garlic cloves**, crushed
2 teaspoons **ground coriander**
1 teaspoon each **ground cumin, ground cinnamon, ground turmeric**
1 large **aubergine**, about 375 g (12 oz), diced
400 g (13 oz) can **chickpeas**, drained
400 g (13 oz) can chopped **tomatoes**
300 ml (½ pint) **vegetable stock**
250 g (8 oz) **button mushrooms**
75 g (3 oz) **dried figs**, chopped
2 tablespoons chopped **coriander**
salt and **black pepper**
preserved lemon, chopped, to garnish

Heat 2 tablespoons of the oil in a saucepan, add the onion, garlic and spices and cook over a medium heat, stirring frequently, for 5 minutes until lightly golden. Heat a further 2 tablespoons of the oil in the pan, add the aubergines and cook, stirring, for 4–5 minutes until browned. Add the chickpeas, tomatoes and stock and bring to the boil. Reduce the heat, cover and simmer gently for 20 minutes.

Meanwhile, heat the remaining oil in a frying pan, add the mushrooms and cook over a medium heat for 4–5 minutes until browned.

Add the mushrooms to the tagine with the figs and cook for a further 10 minutes. Stir in the coriander. Garnish with chopped preserved lemon.

For butternut squash tagine, soften 2 sliced onions in 2 tablespoons of olive oil in a large pan. Stir in 2 teaspoons each of ground cumin and coriander and 2 crushed garlic cloves and cook for 2 minutes, then add 2 tablespoons of rose harissa and cook for a further 3 minutes. Add 1 butternut squash and 4 carrots, peeled and cut into chunks, and cook, stirring constantly, for 10 minutes. Stir in 75 g (3 oz) chopped dried apricots and pour over 600 ml (1 pint) vegetable stock. Cook gently for 20–25 minutes, or until the vegetables are almost tender. Add a 400 g (13 oz) can of chickpeas and cook for a further 5 minutes. Season to taste with salt and black pepper and stir in 2 tablespoons each of coriander and flat-leaf parsley to serve.

chickpea & potato tagine

Serves **4**
Preparation time **15 minutes**
Cooking time **46 minutes**
Finishing time **10 minutes**

2 tablespoons **sunflower oil**
2 **onions**, roughly chopped
1 teaspoon **smoked paprika**
1 teaspoon **ground turmeric**
2 teaspoons **cumin seeds**,
  roughly crushed
500 g (1 lb) **potatoes**,
  scrubbed and cubed
400 g (13 oz) can **chickpeas**,
  drained
400 g (13 oz) can **pinto
  beans**, drained
100 g (3½ oz) **preserved
  lemons**, drained and
  quartered
600 ml (1 pint) **vegetable
  stock**
small bunch of **coriander**
125 g (4 oz) **feta cheese**,
  crumbled (optional)
salt and **pepper**

Heat the oil in a saucepan, add the onion and fry for 5 minutes until lightly browned. Stir in the spices and cook for 1 minute. Mix in the potatoes and drained pulses and stir well.

Add the preserved lemons, stock and seasoning. Bring to the boil then reduce the heat, cover and simmer gently for 40 minutes until the potatoes are tender. Allow to cool, then chill until required.

To serve, reheat the potato mixture on the hob, stirring occasionally and topping up with a little water if needed until piping hot. Spoon into shallow bowls and top with torn coriander leaves and feta cheese, if using. Serve with warmed pitta or flat Arab breads, if liked.

For lentil & fennel tagine, gently soften 12 peeled baby shallots in 2 tablespoons of olive oil. Add 150 g (5 oz) green lentils, 125 g (4 oz) chopped dried apricots, 2 crushed garlic cloves, a 4 cm (1½ inch) piece of fresh ginger, finely grated, 2 teaspoons of ras-el-hanout and ½ teaspoon of ground cumin. Cook for a further 2 minutes, then pour over 900 ml (1½ pints) vegetable stock. Bring to the boil, then cover and simmer over a low heat for 15 minutes. Add 150 g (5 oz) baby carrots, 2 fennel bulbs cut into wedges, and 2 sliced courgettes and cook for a further 5 minutes. Add 200 g (7 oz) fresh peas and the grated rind of 1 lemon and cook for a further 5 minutes. Stir in the juice of 1 lemon and season to taste with salt and black pepper.

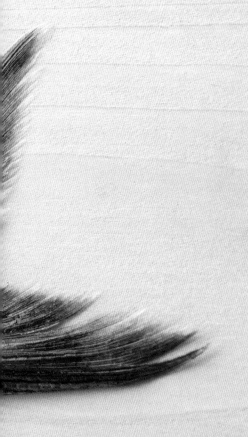

fish

spliced sardines

Serves **6**
Preparation time **15 minutes**,
   plus marinating
Cooking time **15 minutes**

36 **sardines**
4 **garlic cloves**
½ bunch of **flat-leaf parsley**
1 large bunch of **coriander**
1 **lemon**, juiced
1 tablespoon **paprika**
1 tablespoon **ground cumin**
pinch of **cayenne pepper**
100 g (3½ oz) **plain flour**
½ teaspoon **salt**
oil for frying
lemon wedges, to serve

Fillet and butterfly the sardines (or ask your fishmonger to do this when you buy them).

Rinse the sardines and let them drain while you prepare the marinade. Chop the garlic, parsley and coriander, tip into a large bowl, and add the lemon juice, salt and the spices.

Coat the fillets with marinade on both sides, then press them together in pairs, open sides together. Lay on a plate, drizzle over the remaining marinade, cover with clingfilm, and marinate in the refrigerator for 1 hour.

Heat the oil in a large frying pan, dredge the sardines with flour on both sides, and fry over low heat, turning once. Transfer to kitchen paper to absorb the excess oil before arranging on a serving platter.

For sardine balls with chermoula, mix together 125 ml (4 fl oz) olive oil, the juice of 1 lemon, 4 tablespoons each of chopped flat-leaf parsley and coriander, 4 crushed garlic cloves, 1 teaspoon each of ground cumin and paprika and salt and black pepper to taste, for the chermoula. Finely chop 1 kg (2 lb) sardine fillets in a food processor, then mix with 2 tablespoons of cooked rice and enough chermoula to bind. Form the mixture into little balls. Simmer 6 peeled and chopped ripe tomatoes with the remaining chermoula and a bay leaf, until reduced. Add the sardine balls and 2 tablespoons of water and cook, stirring occasionally, for a further 15 minutes.

stuffed squid

Serves **6**
Preparation time **15 minutes**
Cooking time **20 minutes**

6 medium **squid** (about
   12 cm/5 inches long)
1 bunch of **flat-leaf parsley**
1 bunch of **coriander**
5 oz (150 g) **minced beef**
100 g (3½ oz) **cooked rice**
¼ teaspoon **pepper**
1 tablespoon **paprika**
100 ml (3½ fl oz) **passata**
   (sieved tomatoes)
2 tablespoons **olive oil**
2 **garlic cloves**, sliced
¼ teaspoon **ground cumin**
200 ml (7 fl oz) **water**
½ teaspoon **tomato paste**
salt

Wash and clean the squid and set aside. Wash and snip the parsley and coriander separately.

Mix together the meat, parsley, rice, salt to taste, pepper and half the paprika in a large bowl.

Stuff the squid pouches and secure with a toothpick.

Put the passata into a large casserole with the oil, garlic, coriander, cumin and the remaining paprika. Pour in the water and bring to a simmer. Add the squid and the tomato paste, cover, and simmer for 20 minutes. The squid should be tender and the sauce reduced.

For squid with prawns & harissa, clean the squid, cut into thin strips and season to taste with salt and black pepper. Fry with 500 g (1 lb) raw prawns in 6 tablespoons of olive oil over a high heat, stirring occasionally, for about 1 minute, or until the squid is just opaque and the prawns are pink. Stir in 6 tablespoons of harissa (see page 76) and 4 tablespoons of chopped coriander and serve immediately.

prawns 'pil-pil'

Serves **6**
Preparation time **5 minutes**
Cooking time **10 minutes**

4 tablespoons **groundnut oil**
500 g (1 lb) raw **tiger prawns**,
  shelled and deveined
2 **garlic cloves**, roughly
  chopped
1 tablespoon snipped **flat-leaf
  parsley**
½ teaspoon **paprika**
½ teaspoon **salt**
2 fresh **red chilli peppers**, to
  garnish

Heat the oil in a frying pan or flameproof tagine over a medium heat.

Add the prawns, garlic, parsley, paprika and salt. Stir gently, turning to cook on both sides, then add the chilli peppers to garnish the dish. Serve hot.

For prawns in tomato sauce, fry a chopped onion in 2 tablespoons of olive oil until just starting to colour. Add 3 finely chopped garlic cloves; when they start to colour, stir in 400 g (10 oz) peeled and chopped tomatoes, ½ teaspoon of ground ginger, a pinch of chilli pepper and a pinch of salt. Simmer for 20 minutes or until the sauce is reduced. Add the prawns, turning to cook on both sides. Season to taste with salt and black pepper, then stir in 1 tablespoon each of chopped parsley and coriander.

fried whiting with chermoula

Serves **6**
Preparation time **15 minutes**,
  plus marinating
Cooking time **15 minutes**

6 whole **whiting** or 12 fillets
1 bunch of **coriander**, snipped
1 bunch of **flat-leaf parsley**,
  snipped
2 **garlic cloves**, crushed
½ teaspoon **sweet paprika**
½ teaspoon **ground cumin**
1 **lemon**, juiced
1 tablespoon **water**
4 tablespoons **flour**
½ teaspoon **salt**
oil, for frying
lemon wedges, to serve

Wash the whole or filleted fish.

Prepare the marinade in a shallow dish by mixing
together the herbs, garlic, spices, lemon juice and water.

Place the fish in the marinade, cover with clingfilm and
leave to marinate for 30 minutes in the refrigerator.

Tip the flour onto a plate and dip in the fish to coat both
sides. Reserve the remaining flour and the marinade.

Heat the oil in a frying pan large enough to
accommodate the whiting and quickly fry the fish,
turning once. You may have to work in batches.

Remove the fish and keep warm. Mix the remaining
flour with the marinade and shape into flat patties.
Fry in the hot oil and serve with the fish.

For deep-fried fish with chermoula sauce, mix the
juice of 1½ lemons with a generous handful of chopped
coriander, 2 crushed garlic cloves, ½ a finely chopped
red chilli pepper, 6 tablespoons of olive oil and salt to
taste. Dip 6 white fish fillets in flour as above and quickly
deep-fry them in batches until golden. Serve hot, with
the sauce poured over.

moroccan fish tagine

Serves **4**
Preparation time **15 minutes**
Cooking time **55 minutes**

750 g (1 ½ lb) **firm white fish
   fillets**, such as cod, sea bass
   or monkfish, pin-boned,
   skinned and cut into 5 cm
   (2 inch) chunks
½ teaspoon **cumin seeds**
½ teaspoon **coriander seeds**
6 **cardamom pods**
4 tablespoons **olive oil**
2 small **onions**, thinly sliced
2 **garlic cloves**, crushed
¼ teaspoon **ground turmeric**
1 **cinnamon stick**
40 g (1 ½ oz) **sultanas**
25 g (1 oz) **pine nuts**, lightly
   toasted
150 ml (¼ pint) **fish stock**
finely grated rind of 1 **lemon**,
   plus 1 tablespoon juice
salt and **pepper**
chopped **parsley**, to garnish

Season the fish with salt and pepper.

Using a pestle and mortar, crush the cumin and
coriander seeds and cardamom pods. Discard the
cardamom pods, leaving the seeds.

Heat the oil in a large, shallow frying pan and fry the
onions gently for 6–8 minutes until golden. Add the
garlic, crushed spices, turmeric and cinnamon and fry
gently, stirring, for 2 minutes. Add the fish pieces, turning
them until they are coated in the oil. Transfer the fish
and onions to an ovenproof casserole dish and scatter
with the sultanas and pine nuts.

Add the stock and lemon rind and juice to the frying
pan and bring the mixture to the boil. Pour the mixture
around the fish, then cover and bake in a preheated
oven, 160°C (325°F), Gas Mark 3, for 40 minutes.
Garnish with parsley before serving.

For pomegranate & coriander couscous to serve as
an accompaniment, bring 400 ml (14 fl oz) vegetable
stock to the boil. Pour it over 300 g (10 oz) couscous in
a heatproof bowl, cover with clingfilm and leave to steam
for 5 minutes, then stir in the seeds of 1 pomegranate
and 2 tablespoons of roughly chopped coriander leaves.
Finally, mix in 2 tablespoons of olive oil and the juice of
½ lemon and season with salt and pepper.

hake with saffron

Serves **6**
Preparation time **10 minutes**
Cooking time **15 minutes**

1 bunch of **coriander**
4 **garlic cloves**
½ teaspoon **ground ginger**
½ teaspoon **ground turmeric**
2 pinches of **saffron threads**
6 **hake steaks**
3 tablespoons **olive oil**
100 ml (3½ fl oz) **water**
1 **tomato**, skinned and
    chopped finely
1 **preserved lemon**, sliced
    into strips
salt
lemon slices, to garnish

Finely mince together the coriander and the garlic.
Put in a bowl with the spices. Coat the fish with the
spice mixture and set aside.

Pour the oil and water into a large casserole. Place
over the heat and bring to a gentle boil before carefully
lowering in the fish. Cook over a low heat for around
15 minutes.

Add the tomato and the preserved lemon to the pan.
When the sauce is thick, remove the pan from the heat
and carefully lift out the fish.

Serve with the sauce spooned on top.

For saffron fish balls, process to a thick paste 500 g
(1 lb) white fish fillets, 1 egg, 2 chopped spring onions,
1 tablespoon each of chopped coriander and flat-leaf
parsley, 50 g (2 oz) fresh white breadcrumbs, a large
pinch of saffron and seasoning to taste. Shape the
mixture into walnut-sized balls and set aside. Fry a finely
chopped onion in 4 tablespoons of olive oil until soft. Stir
in 500 g (1 lb) peeled and chopped tomatoes, 2 crushed
garlic cloves, 1 tablespoon of harissa, 1 teaspoon of
paprika, ½ teaspoon of ground cumin and a pinch of
sugar. Add 250 ml (8 fl oz) water, bring to the boil, then
simmer for 15 minutes. Add the fish balls and simmer,
covered, for a further 15 minutes, shaking the pan
occasionally.

stuffed red sea bream

Serves **6**
Preparation time **15 minutes**
Cooking time **1 hour
5 minutes**

1 whole **sea bream** weighing
about 1.5 kg (3 lb), cleaned,
scaled
14 oz (400 g) **hake fillet**
1 bunch of **flat-leaf parsley**
2 **celery stalks**
1 **red pepper**
1 **preserved lemon**
3 **garlic cloves**
2 tablespoons **sunflower oil**
250 g (8 oz) **cooked rice**
½ teaspoon **ground turmeric**
pinch of **saffron**
½ teaspoon **ground ginger**
1 **lemon**, juiced
2 tablespoons **olive oil**
200 ml (7 fl oz) **water**
pinch of **pepper**
salt

Wash the sea bream thoroughly. Mince together the hake, parsley, celery, pepper, preserved lemon and garlic. Heat 1 tablespoon of the sunflower oil in a frying pan, add the mixture, and cook over a low heat, stirring, for 3 minutes. Remove from the pan and leave to cool.

Put the rice, spices, and half the lemon juice in a bowl, then add the cooled hake mixture and combine.

Preheat the oven to 180°C (350°F), Gas Mark 6.

Rub the sea bream with the remaining lemon juice, season with salt and pepper, and drizzle over the remaining olive oil, then fill with the stuffing. Put the remaining sunflower and olive oil in a shallow ovenproof dish, pour in the water, and place the stuffed fish in the casserole. Transfer to the oven and cook for 1 hour.

For sea bream with new potatoes, mix 6 tablespoons of olive oil with the juice of 1 lemon, 4 tablespoons of chopped coriander, 4 crushed garlic cloves, 1 teaspoon each of ground cumin and paprika and ½ teaspoon of chilli pepper. Sprinkle 6 sea bream fillets with salt and marinate in half the chermoula. Cut 1 kg (2 lb) potatoes into thin slices and 4 large, firm tomatoes into slightly thicker slices. Toss gently in 2 tablespoons of olive oil, season to taste, then transfer to an oiled ovenproof dish. Bake in a preheated oven, 240°C (475°F), Gas Mark 9, turning occasionally, for about 45 minutes until tender. Place the fish fillets on top, skin side up, and bake for a further 10 minutes, or until the fish is cooked. Serve drizzled with the remaining chermoula.

sea bass with celery

Serves 6
Preparation time **15 minutes**
Cooking time **1 hour**

1 whole **sea bass**, weighing
   about 1.5 kg (3 lb), cleaned
   and scaled
1 head of **celery**
300 ml (½ pint) **passata**
   (sieved tomatoes)
½ teaspoon **sweet paprika**
½ teaspoon **pepper**
4 tablespoons **olive oil**
3 **garlic cloves**
250 ml (8 fl oz) **water**
salt
couscous, to serve

Wash the sea bass thoroughly and set aside. Separate and wash the celery stalks, reserving the leafy parts. Remove the strings and cut the stalks into pieces about 4 cm (1½ inches) in length. Bring a large pan of salted water to the boil and blanch the celery for 2 minutes. Meanwhile, finely chop the reserved leafy parts.

Put the passata into a frying pan with the paprika, pepper, a little salt and half the olive oil. Heat gently for 10 minutes, then add the blanched celery and leafy parts and continue to cook for a further 10 minutes. Remove from the heat and allow to cool.

Preheat the oven to 180°C (350°F), Gas Mark 6.

Put half the tomato sauce in the base of an ovenproof dish that will accommodate the fish and place the sea bass on top. Drizzle over the remaining olive oil and the rest of the sauce, then add the water. Mix well, then cook in the preheated oven for around 45 minutes. Serve with couscous.

For sea bass with herbs, make the tomato sauce as above, omitting the paprika. Mix together 6 tablespoons each of chopped coriander and flat-leaf parsley, 3 crushed garlic cloves and the finely grated rind and juice of 1½ lemons. Season to taste with salt and black pepper and use to stuff the fish. Cook the fish with the sauce as above.

sea bream with olives

Serves **6**
Preparation time **20 minutes**
Cooking time **1 hour**

1 whole **sea bream**, weighing
about 2 kg (4 lb), cleaned
and scaled
3 **tomatoes**, skinned and cut
into small pieces
3 **celery stalks**, finely chopped
1 bunch of **flat-leaf parsley**,
finely chopped
2 **preserved lemons**,
quartered, pulp removed,
and rind finely sliced
3 **garlic cloves**, minced
5 **potatoes**, sliced
½ teaspoon **turmeric**
½ teaspoon **pepper**
250 g (8 oz) **cooked rice**
250 g (8 oz) **green olives**,
pitted
3 tablespoons **olive oil**
salt

Wash the fish thoroughly, then slash twice on both sides.

Prepare a marinade with the tomatoes, celery, parsley, lemon rind, garlic, turmeric, pepper, salt to taste and a large glass of water. Add half the mixture to the cooked rice with half the olives. Fill the fish cavity with this stuffing.

Preheat the oven to 180°C (350°F), Gas Mark 6.

Pour the oil and the remaining marinade into a roasting tin and place the fish in the middle with the sliced potatoes around it. Stir well to coat the potatoes in the marinade. Transfer to the oven and cook for 1 hour. Serve garnished with the remaining olives.

For skate with olives, heat 6 tablespoons of olive oil in a large frying pan and gently cook 6 small skate wings on one side for 4 minutes. Turn the fish over and continue cooking until the flesh is opaque and readily comes away from the bones. Remove from the pan and keep warm. (Do this in two batches if necessary.) Stir into the pan the juice of 1 ½ lemons, the chopped peel of 2 small preserved lemons, 18 pitted and chopped green olives and 3 tablespoons of chopped coriander. Heat through gently and pour over the fish to serve.

moroccan grilled sardines

Serves **4**
Preparation time **10 minutes**
Cooking time **6–8 minutes**

12 **sardines**, cleaned and
  gutted
2 tablespoons **harissa**
2 tablespoons **olive oil**
1 **lemon**, juiced
salt flakes and **pepper**
chopped **coriander**, to garnish
lemon wedges, to serve

Heat the grill on the hottest setting. Rinse the sardines and pat dry with kitchen paper. Make 3 deep slashes on both sides of each fish with a sharp knife.

Mix the harissa with the oil and lemon juice to make a thin paste. Rub into the sardines on both sides. Put the sardines on a lightly oiled baking sheet. Cook under the grill for 3–4 minutes on each side, depending on their size, or until cooked through.

Season to taste with salt flakes and pepper and serve immediately garnished with coriander and with lemon wedges for squeezing over.

For baked sardines with pesto, line a medium ovenproof dish with 2 sliced tomatoes and 2 sliced onions. Prepare the sardines as above, then rub 4 tablespoons of pesto over the fish and arrange in a single layer on top of the tomatoes and onions. Cover with foil and bake in a preheated oven, 200°C (400°F), Gas Mark 6, for 20–25 minutes or until the fish is cooked through.

tangiers-style anchovies

Serves **6**
Preparation time **35 minutes**
Cooking time **10 minutes**

1 kg (2 lb) **anchovies**
6 **garlic cloves**, chopped
1 bunch of **flat-leaf parsley**,
　finely chopped
1 bunch of **coriander**, finely
　chopped
2 tablespoons **paprika**
2 tablespoons **ground cumin**
4 tablespoons **vinegar**
2 tablespoons **water**
4 tablespoons **olive oil**
2 tablespoons ground **thyme
leaves**

Wash the anchovies and remove the spine to make two fillets without separating them. Lay them flat in a bowl.

Preheat the oven to 180°C (350°F), Gas Mark 6.

Prepare a marinade with all the ingredients except the olive oil and ground thyme. Dip each prepared anchovy on both sides first in the marinade, then in the olive oil. Close the two fillets together, and arrange them in a single layer in a roasting tin or tagine. Pour the remaining marinade over the anchovies and sprinkle with the thyme.

Transfer the tin to the oven for 10 minutes or place the tagine over a very low heat.

For roasted peppers with anchovies, place 6 halved and deseeded red peppers in an ovenproof dish and coat all over with olive oil. Arrange cut side up and roast in a preheated oven, 160°F (325°F), Gas Mark 3, for 35–40 minutes or until softened. Fill each pepper half with ½ a tomato, 2 or 3 slices of garlic, ¼ teaspoon of finely chopped preserved lemon, a sprig of rosemary and 2 anchovies, split lengthways. Drizzle the peppers with olive oil and return to the oven for a further 30 minutes or until the tomatoes are soft. Serve at room temperature.

kebabs & accompaniments

beef kebabs

Serves **6**

Preparation time **15 minutes**,
  plus resting

Cooking time **5 minutes**

1.2 kg (2¼ lb) **fillet of beef**,
  cubed
1 large **onion**, chopped
1 bunch of **flat-leaf parsley**,
  snipped
¼ teaspoon **pepper**
salt

Mix together all the ingredients in a bowl and season
with salt.

Cover with clingfilm and place in the refrigerator for
1 hour.

Thread the beef onto 6 skewers and cook for
5 minutes, turning regularly, over hot coals or under
a hot grill.

For sweet tomato sauce to serve as an accompaniment,
gently heat 2 tablespoons of olive oil with 2 sliced garlic
cloves for 3 minutes. Remove the garlic and add
1 kg (2 lb) peeled and chopped ripe tomatoes, a pinch
of salt and 1 tablespoon of sugar. Cook over a low heat
for 45–60 minutes, stirring frequently, until the liquid
has evaporated and the sauce has thickened. Stir in
½ teaspoon of ground cinnamon and 1 tablespoon of
honey and season generously with black pepper. Cook
for a further minute and serve hot with the kebabs.

calves' liver kebabs

Serves **6**
Preparation time **15 minutes**,
  plus resting
Cooking time **8 minutes**

1 kg (2 lb) **calves' liver**, thickly
  sliced
150 g (5 oz) **beef caul fat**
1 teaspoon **ground cumin**
1 tablespoon **paprika**
¼ teaspoon **pepper**
salt
chipped **potatoes**, to serve

Grill the liver slices quickly on both sides.

Cut the liver and caul fat into pieces and put in a bowl
with the spices and salt. Cover with clingfilm and place
in the refrigerator for 1 hour.

Thread the liver onto 6 skewers, alternating with two
pieces of fat on each skewer, and cook for 8 minutes,
turning regularly, over hot coals or under a hot grill.

Serve with chipped potatoes.

For carrot & spinach salad to serve as an
accompaniment, heat 1 tablespoon of olive oil in a
saucepan, then add 6 diagonally sliced carrots, the
juice of 2 lemons, 4 teaspoons of sugar and a large
pinch of salt. Cover and cook over a low heat until the
carrots are just tender, adding a little water if necessary.
Meanwhile, steam 250 g (8 oz) spinach until just wilted,
then drain thoroughly and roughly chop. Toss the carrots
and spinach in a dressing of 1 tablespoon of olive oil,
4 teaspoons of orange juice, ½ teaspoon of sugar,
½ teaspoon of ground cumin and 2 chopped garlic
cloves. Serve warm.

meatball kebabs

Serves **6**
Preparation time **25 minutes**
Cooking time **3 minutes**

1 large **onion**
1 bunch of **flat-leaf parsley**
1 bunch of **coriander**
1 **mint stalk**
1 kg (2 lb) **minced beef**
1 tablespoon **paprika**
1 teaspoon **ground cumin**
pinch of **ras-el-hanout**
salt
chopped **salad vegetables**,
  to serve

Finely mince the onion and herbs together. Transfer to a bowl with the beef, spices and salt to taste and mix thoroughly.

Form into 24 balls each about 4 cm (1½ inches) across, then flatten slightly and thread onto 6 skewers, four to a skewer. (You can also flatten them completely to form small burgers.)

Cook for 5 minutes, turning regularly, over hot coals or under a hot grill.

Serve with a chopped, mixed salad.

For moroccan taktouka-style cooked salad to serve as an accompaniment, cut 3 large ripe tomatoes into chunks and place them in a pan with 2 chopped onions, ½ a cucumber halved lengthways, deseeded and sliced, and 1 green pepper and 1 red pepper, deseeded and chopped. Add 6 tablespoons of boiling water and simmer over low heat for 5 minutes to soften the vegetables. Cool and drain, then toss very gently in a dressing made from the juice of 1 lemon, 3 tablespoons of olive oil, 2 crushed garlic cloves, 2 tablespoons of chopped coriander and salt and black pepper to taste.

lamb kebabs

Serves **6**

Preparation time **15 minutes**, plus resting

Cooking time **5 minutes**

1 kg (2 lb) boned **leg of lamb**, cubed

1 **onion**, roughly chopped

1 bunch of **flat-leaf parsley**, snipped

1 teaspoon **ground cumin**

1 tablespoon **paprika**

¼ teaspoon **pepper**

salt

3 **flatbreads**, cut in half, to serve

Mix together all the ingredients in a bowl, season with salt, then cover with clingfilm and place in the refrigerator for 2 hours.

Thread the lamb onto 6 skewers and cook for 5 minutes, turning regularly, over hot coals or under a hot grill.

Open out the flatbread halves, insert the meat pieces and serve.

For home-made flatbreads, stir ½ teaspoon of dried yeast into 250 ml (8 fl oz) warm water. Place 500 g (1 lb) plain flour in a large bowl, make a well in the centre and pour in 4 tablespoons of olive oil and the yeast mixture. Using your hands, work the flour into the liquid to make a dough. Knead until smooth and elastic, then set aside in a warm place for 1½ hours. Turn out the dough and divide it into 6 pieces. Roll each piece out thinly, sprinkle with sea salt flakes and cook on lightly oiled baking sheets in a preheated oven, 220°C (425°F), Gas Mark 7, for about 8 minutes, or until golden.

beef & pepper kebabs

Serves **4**

Preparation time **15 minutes**,
plus marinating

Cooking time **15 minutes**

400 g (13 oz) **steak**, rump or
topside

1 **red pepper**, cored and
deseeded

1 **green pepper**, cored and
deseeded

1 teaspoon crushed **coriander
seeds**

3 tablespoons **vegetable oil**

15 g (½ oz) **coriander**,
chopped

1 **red chilli**, deseeded and
chopped

1 **garlic clove**, crushed

2 tablespoons **lime juice**

4 **chapattis**

salt and **pepper**

Presoak 8 wooden skewers in warm water. Cut the beef
and peppers into 2.5 cm (1 inch) cubes.

Mix together the coriander seeds, 2 tablespoons of oil
and half the chopped coriander in a bowl and season to
taste. Add the beef and peppers and toss to coat.

Thread the beef and peppers onto the skewers, cover
and refrigerate for up to 1 hour.

Mix together the remaining coriander and oil with the
chilli, garlic and lime juice to make a dressing, season to
taste and set aside.

Grill the skewers under a preheated hot grill for
15 minutes, turning often and basting with the juices.
Warm the chapattis under the grill.

Serve 2 skewers per person on a hot chapatti and
drizzle over the coriander dressing.

For moroccan lettuce salad to serve as an
accompaniment, shred the outer leaves of 2 romaine
lettuce hearts and separate the smaller inner leaves.
Place the shredded lettuce and whole leaves in a
bowl and add 1 finely sliced red onion. Pour over the
juice of 1 lemon and 2 tablespoons of olive oil, season
generously with sea salt and black pepper, and toss the
salad thoroughly.

marinated minty lamb kebabs

Serves **4**
Preparation time **15 minutes**,
  plus marinating
Cooking time **10 minutes**

1 **garlic clove**, crushed
2 tablespoons chopped **mint**
1 tablespoon ready-made **mint
  sauce**
150 g (5 oz) **natural yogurt**
375 g (12 oz) lean **lamb**,
  cubed
2 small **onions**, cut into
  wedges
1 **green pepper**, cored,
  deseeded and cut into
  wedges
lemon wedges, green salad
  and couscous, to serve

Mix together the garlic, mint, mint sauce and yogurt in
a medium bowl, add the lamb and stir well. Cover and
leave to marinate in a cool place for 10 minutes.

Thread the lamb and onion and pepper wedges onto
8 metal skewers and cook under a preheated hot grill
for 8—10 minutes or until cooked through.

Serve the kebabs with lemon wedges and, if liked,
accompany them with a green salad and couscous.

For spicy lamb kebabs with ginger, marinate the lamb
in a mixture of 5 cm (2 inches) fresh root ginger, peeled
and finely grated, 4 tablespoons each of soy sauce and
dry sherry, 1 teaspoon of caster sugar and 1 tablespoon
of lemon juice. Grill as above.

chicken skewers with couscous

Serves **4**
Preparation time **25 minutes**,
    plus chilling
Cooking time **20–25 minutes**

500 g (1 lb) boneless, skinless
    chicken breasts
2 tablespoons **olive oil**
2 **garlic cloves**, crushed
½ teaspoon each **ground
    cumin, turmeric, paprika**
2 teaspoons **lemon juice**

Couscous
4 tablespoons **olive oil**
1 small **onion**, finely chopped
1 **garlic clove**, crushed
1 teaspoon each **ground cumin,
    cinnamon, pepper, ginger**
50 g (2 oz) each **dried dates,
    dried apricots**, blanched
    almonds, toasted
600 ml (1 pint) **vegetable
    stock**, boiling
175 g (6 oz) **couscous**
1 tablespoon **lemon juice**
2 tablespoons chopped
    coriander leaves
salt and **pepper**
pomegranate seeds, lemon
    wedges, **coriander** sprigs, to
    garnish

Cut the chicken into long thin strips, place in a shallow dish and add the olive oil, garlic, spices and lemon juice. Stir well, cover and leave to marinate for 2 hours. Thread the chicken strips on to 8 presoaked wooden skewers.

Prepare the couscous by heating half the oil in a saucepan and frying the onion, garlic and spices for 5 minutes. Chop and stir in the dried fruits and almonds and remove from the heat.

Meanwhile, put the couscous in a heatproof bowl, add the boiling stock, cover with a tea towel and steam for 8–10 minutes, until all the liquid is absorbed. Stir in the remaining oil and the fruit and nut mixture, add the lemon juice and coriander and season to taste.

While the couscous is steaming, grill the chicken skewers for 4–5 minutes on each side, until charred and cooked through. Serve with the couscous, garnished with pomegranate seeds, lemon wedges and coriander sprigs, if liked.

For roasted chicken with herb couscous, mix the oil, garlic, spices and lemon juice and drizzle over 8 skinned and slashed chicken thighs. Roast at 190°C (375°F), Gas Mark 5, for 35–45 minutes. Steam the couscous as above in stock. Stir in the remaining oil and lemon juice. Add 4 finely chopped spring onions, 3 tablespoons of chopped mint, 3 tablespoons of chopped parsley and 2 chopped tomatoes. Spoon onto plates, top with the chicken and serve with lemon wedges.

vegetables

potatoes 'mchermel'

Serves **6**
Preparation time **15 minutes**
Cooking time **20 minutes**

1 kg (2 lb) **potatoes**
1 bunch of **flat-leaf parsley**
1 bunch of **coriander**
3 **garlic cloves**
3 tablespoons **olive oil**
1 tablespoon **paprika**
½ teaspoon **ground cumin**
pinch of **cayenne pepper**
300 ml (½ pint) **water**
salt

Peel and wash the potatoes, then cut into medium-sized pieces. Chop the herbs and garlic together.

Heat the oil in a heavy-based casserole. Add the chopped herbs and garlic, cook for 2 minutes, then add the potatoes.

Cook for 3 minutes, add the spices and salt to taste, then pour in the water. Cover the pan, lower the heat, and cook for 15 minutes until the sauce has reduced.

For potatoes with fennel, place 3 tablespoons of olive oil in a pan with 625 g (1¼ lb) halved new potatoes. Place 3 trimmed and quartered fennel bulbs on top with 3 sliced garlic cloves. Season to taste with salt and black pepper, then cover with water, bring to the boil and simmer, covered, for 15 minutes. Add 4 tablespoons each of chopped mint and basil, then cook, uncovered, for a further 10 minutes until the vegetables are tender and the sauce is reduced. Stir in 2 tablespoons of lemon juice and serve drizzled with olive oil.

green lentils in tomato sauce

Serves **6**
Preparation time **15 minutes**
Cooking time **25 minutes**

3 tablespoons **olive oil**
1 **onion**, chopped
2 **garlic cloves**, chopped
3 **tomatoes**, skinned and
   crushed
200 ml (7 fl oz) **water**
½ teaspoon **tomato paste**
500 g (1 lb) **green lentils**
½ teaspoon **paprika**
1 **red pepper**, cored, deseeded
   and roughly chopped
1 bunch **flat-leaf parsley**
salt and **pepper**

Heat the oil in a heavy-based casserole, add the onion, garlic and tomatoes and cook for 10 minutes.

Add the water, stir in the tomato paste, then add the lentils, paprika and salt and pepper to taste.

Add the pepper and the parsley to the pan and continue to cook over a low heat for 10 minutes until the sauce has reduced.

For lentils with cumin, heat 2 tablespoons of oil and gently fry 2 sliced onions and 4 chopped garlic cloves until softened. Stir in 500 g (1 lb) green lentils, 4 teaspoons of crushed cumin seeds and 2 teaspoons of crushed coriander seeds. Pour over 200 ml (7 fl oz) water and cook over a low heat for 20–25 minutes, until the lentils are tender. Stir in 1 tablespoon of lemon juice and season to taste with salt and black pepper.

saffron-scented vegetable tagine

Serves **4**
Preparation time **15 minutes**
Cooking time **50 minutes**

100 ml (3½ fl oz) **sunflower oil**
1 large **onion**, finely chopped
2 **garlic cloves**, crushed
2 teaspoons each **ground coriander, cumin, cinnamon**
400 g (13 oz) can **chickpeas**, drained
400 g (13 oz) can chopped **tomatoes**
600 ml (1 pint) **vegetable stock**
¼ teaspoon **saffron threads**
1 large **aubergine**, trimmed and chopped
250 g (8 oz) **button mushrooms**, trimmed and halved if large
100 g (3½ oz) **dried figs**, chopped
2 tablespoons chopped fresh **coriander**
salt and **black** pepper
steamed **couscous**, to serve

Heat 2 tablespoons of the oil in a frying pan, add the onion, garlic and spices and cook over a medium heat, stirring frequently, for 5 minutes until golden. Using a slotted spoon, transfer to a saucepan and add the chickpeas, tomatoes, stock and saffron. Season with salt and pepper.

Heat the remaining oil in the frying pan, add the aubergine and cook over a high heat, stirring frequently, for 5 minutes until browned. Add to the stew and bring to the boil, then reduce the heat, cover and simmer gently for 20 minutes.

Stir in the mushrooms and figs and simmer gently, uncovered, for a further 20 minutes. Stir in the fresh coriander and adjust the seasoning. Serve with steamed couscous.

For winter vegetable & lentil tagine, replace the aubergine with 2 sliced carrots and 2 cubed potatoes. Instead of the chickpeas, use a drained 400 g (13 oz) can of green lentils. Follow the recipe above and stir in 100 g (3½ oz) dried apricots instead of the figs.

courgettes with tomatoes

Serves **6**
Preparation time **10 minutes**
Cooking time **20 minutes**

3 tablespoons **olive oil**
1 **onion**, finely sliced
3 **tomatoes**, diced
3 **garlic cloves**
1 tablespoon **paprika**
250 ml (8 fl oz) **water**
1 kg (2 lb) **courgettes**,
   trimmed and cut into rounds,
   then halved or quartered
salt

Heat the oil in a heavy-based casserole, add the onion and tomatoes and soften for 5 minutes. Add the garlic, paprika and salt to taste and pour in the water.

When the sauce is simmering, add the courgettes and cook for 15 minutes.

Remove from the heat once the sauce has reduced.

For okra with tomatoes, heat 4 tablespoons of olive oil and fry 3 thinly sliced onions with 3 teaspoons of crushed coriander seeds for about 4 minutes, until starting to colour. Add 750 g (1½ lb) trimmed whole okra and 4 crushed garlic cloves and fry for a further 1 minute. Stir in 750 g (1½ lb) peeled and chopped tomatoes and 1 teaspoon of sugar and simmer over a low heat, stirring occasionally, until the okra is tender and the sauce has reduced. Stir in 2 teaspoons of finely grated lemon rind and 3 tablespoons of lemon juice and season to taste with salt and black pepper.

white haricot beans in tomato sauce

Serves **6**
Preparation time **10 minutes**
Cooking time **30 minutes**

2 **tomatoes**, skinned
1 small **onion**
2 **garlic cloves**
3 tablespoons **olive oil**
200 ml (7 fl oz) **water**
500 g (1 lb) canned **white haricot beans**, drained
½ **lemon**, juiced
½ bunch of **flat-leaf parsley**, snipped
½ bunch of **coriander**, snipped
½ teaspoon **sweet paprika**
½ teaspoon **ground ginger**
¼ teaspoon **ground turmeric**
salt

Blend the tomatoes, onion and garlic. Heat the oil in a heavy-based casserole, add the blended vegetables and cook gently for 10 minutes until the mixture has reduced. Pour in the water, allow to return to a simmer, then add the beans.

Simmer for 15 minutes, then add the lemon juice, herbs and spices. Season lightly with salt. Leave over a gentle heat for a further 5 minutes, then serve warm.

For chickpeas in tomato sauce, fry 1 large sliced onion, 2 crushed garlic cloves, 4 chopped dried apricots, 1½ teaspoons of ras-el-hanout, ½ a cinnamon stick, a pinch of red chilli flakes and salt and pepper to taste in 3 tablespoons of olive oil for 7–8 minutes, stirring occasionally, to soften the onion. Add 2 x 400 g (13 oz) cans of chickpeas, drained, and a 400 g (13 oz) can of chopped tomatoes. Bring to the boil and simmer for 5 minutes, until the sauce has reduced. Add the finely grated rind and juice of ½ a lemon, 4 tablespoons of chopped coriander and 1 tablespoon of chopped mint. Cook for a further 5 minutes, then serve warm.

bissara (split pea dip)

Serves **6**
Preparation time **10 minutes**
Cooking time **20 minutes**

Dip
500 g (1 lb) **split peas**
1 **turnip**, peeled and chopped
2 **garlic cloves**
pinch of **salt**

To serve
1 **lemon**, juiced
6 pinches of **ground cumin**
6 pinches of **sweet paprika**
3 teaspoons **olive oil**
warm crusty **bread**

Put the ingredients into a heavy-based casserole with a pinch of salt. Cover with water, then bring to the boil, cover the pan and simmer over a low heat for 50 minutes or until the peas are tender, adding more boiling water if necessary during cooking.

Tip into a blender or rub through a food-mill to create a smooth purée.

Serve in individual dishes with a few drops of lemon juice, a pinch of spices and a little olive oil, accompanied by some warm crusty bread.

For broad bean bissara, place 500 g (1 lb) soaked and drained dried broad beans in a pan with 4 garlic cloves and 2 teaspoons of cumin seeds. Cover with water, then bring to the boil, cover the pan and simmer over a low heat for about 1 hour or until the beans are tender, adding more boiling water if necessary during cooking. Drain the beans, reserving the liquid, and place in a food processor with 150 ml (¼ pint) olive oil, the juice of 3 lemons, 4 tablespoons of the reserved cooking liquid and 1 teaspoon each of paprika and cayenne pepper. Process to a smooth, thin purée, adding a little more of the reserved cooking liquid if necessary. Season with salt to taste and serve warm, drizzled with extra olive oil.

COUSCOUS

grilled vegetables & couscous

Serves **4**
Preparation time **20 minutes**
Cooking time **16–20 minutes**

1 large **aubergine**
2 large **courgettes**
2 **red peppers**, cored,
    deseeded and quartered
4 tablespoons **olive oil**
200 g (7 oz) **couscous**
450 ml (¾ pint) boiling
    vegetable stock
50 g (2 oz) **butter**
2 tablespoons chopped
    mixed herbs, such as mint,
    coriander and parsley
1 **lemon,** juiced
salt and **black pepper**

Tahini yogurt sauce
125 g (4 oz) **Greek-style
    yogurt**
1 tablespoon **tahini paste**
1 **garlic clove**, crushed
½ tablespoon **lemon juice**
1 tablespoon **extra-virgin
    olive oil**

Cut the aubergine and courgettes into 5 mm (¼ inch) thick slices and put in a large bowl with the red peppers. Add the olive oil and salt and pepper and stir well.

Heat a ridged griddle pan until hot. Add the vegetables, in batches, and cook for 3–4 minutes on each side, depending on size, until charred and tender.

Meanwhile, prepare the couscous. Put the couscous in a heatproof bowl. Pour over the boiling stock, cover and leave to soak for 5 minutes. Fluff up the grains with a fork and stir in the butter, herbs, lemon juice and salt and pepper to taste.

Make the tahini yogurt sauce by combining all the ingredients in a bowl and season with salt and pepper. Serve with the vegetables and couscous.

For garlic mayonnaise to serve instead of the tahini yogurt sauce, crush 1–2 garlic cloves and stir into 150 g (5 oz) good-quality mayonnaise. Serve with the vegetables and couscous.

couscous with raisins & chickpeas

Serves **6**
Preparation time **15 minutes**
Cooking time **30 minutes**

75 g (3 oz) **butter**
4 tablespoons **olive oil**
1.5 kg (3 lb) boned **shoulder
   of lamb**, cubed
4 **onions**, finely chopped
200 g (7 oz) **chickpeas**
   (soaked overnight if using
   dried)
½ teaspoon **ground ginger**
½ teaspoon **ground turmeric**
pinch of **saffron**
½ teaspoon **pepper**
½ teaspoon **salt**
1 litre (1¾ pints) **water**
400 g (13 oz) **raisins**
500 g (1 lb) medium-grain
   couscous

Heat half the butter and the oil in a couscous steamer.
Add the meat and onion. When the meat is browned on
all sides, add the chickpeas and the spices and salt.

Pour in the water, cover, and leave to cook for
20 minutes. Add the raisins and cook for a further
5 minutes.

Meanwhile, prepare the couscous following the method
on pages 12–13.

Transfer the couscous to a large, shallow serving dish,
arrange the meat in the centre, and top with the broth,
raisins and chickpeas.

For vegetable & chickpea couscous, soften a
finely chopped onion and 2 crushed garlic cloves in
3 tablespoons of olive oil. Add 1 tablespoon of tomato
purée, ½ teaspoon each of cayenne pepper and
turmeric and 1 teaspoon each of ground coriander
and cumin and cook, stirring, for 2 minutes. Stir in
225 g (8 oz) cauliflower florets, a diced red pepper and
250 ml (8 fl oz) water. Bring to the boil, then simmer for
10 minutes. Add 4 peeled and chopped ripe tomatoes,
2 sliced courgettes and a 400 g (13 oz) can of
chickpeas, rinsed and drained. Cook for a further
10 minutes. Season to taste and serve with the
couscous, garnished with coriander sprigs.

chicken couscous salad

Serves **4**

Preparation time **20 minutes**, plus marinating

Cooking time **20 minutes**

4 boneless, skinless **chicken breasts**, each about 125 g (4 oz)

300 g (10 oz) **couscous**

300 ml (½ pint) hot **chicken stock**

1 **pomegranate**

rind and juice of 1 **orange**

small bunch of **coriander**

small bunch of **mint**

Marinade

1½ tablespoons **curry paste** (tikka masala)

5 tablespoons **natural yogurt**

1 teaspoon **olive oil**

2 tablespoons **lemon juice**

Make the marinade by mixing the curry paste, yogurt and oil. Put the chicken in a non-metallic dish, cover with half the marinade and leave for at least 1 hour.

Put the couscous in a bowl, add the hot stock, cover and leave for 8 minutes.

Meanwhile, cut the pomegranate in half and remove the seeds. Add them to the couscous with the orange rind and juice.

Remove the chicken from the marinade, reserving the marinade, and transfer to a foil-lined baking sheet. Cook in a preheated oven, 190°C (375°F), Gas Mark 5, for 6—7 minutes, then transfer to a preheated hot grill and cook for 2 minutes until caramelized. Cover with foil and leave to rest for 5 minutes.

Chop the coriander and mint roughly, reserving some whole coriander leaves for garnish, and add to the couscous. Thinly slice the chicken. Spoon the couscous onto plates and add the chicken. Thin the reserved marinade with the lemon juice and drizzle over the couscous. Garnish with the reserved coriander leaves and serve immediately.

For pomegranate vinaigrette, an alternative dressing for this salad, whisk together 150 ml (¼ pint) pomegranate juice, 2 tablespoons pomegranate molasses (available from Middle Eastern stores and some supermarkets), 2 tablespoons red wine vinegar and 3 tablespoons olive oil.

sweet couscous with raisins

Serves **6**
Preparation time **20 minutes**
Cooking time **30 minutes**

150 g (5 oz) **butter**
2 tablespoons **olive oil**
4 **onions**, finely chopped
1 large **chicken**, preferably
   free-range, weighing about
   1.8 kg (3½ lb), cut into
   pieces
1 **cinnamon stick**
½ teaspoon **ground ginger**
½ teaspoon **ground turmeric**
pinch of **saffron**
½ teaspoon **pepper**
1 tablespoon **salt**
500 g (1 lb) **raisins**
2 tablespoons **caster sugar**
2 tablespoons **honey**
1 tablespoon **ground**
   cinnamon
500 g (1 lb) medium-grain
   couscous

Heat two-thirds of the butter and the oil in a heavy-based casserole or couscous steamer. Add the onions and allow to soften.

Add the chicken pieces, cinnamon stick, spices and salt. Pour in enough water to cover and leave to cook for 20 minutes. Remove the onions with a slotted spoon.

Put 2 ladlefuls of the broth in a small saucepan with the raisins, sugar, honey and ground cinnamon. Simmer for 5 minutes.

Meanwhile, prepare the couscous following the method on pages 12–13.

Arrange the chicken pieces in a serving dish, surround with the couscous, and top with the spicy raisins.

For sweet vegetable couscous, gently fry 1 sliced red onion, 1 crushed garlic clove and 1 chopped red chilli in 2 tablespoons of olive oil for 5 minutes, then stir in ½ teaspoon each of ground ginger and cinnamon and cook for a further 2 minutes. Add a 400 g (13 oz) can of chopped tomatoes, 4 sliced carrots, 2 cubed turnips, 50 g (2 oz) raisins and 225 ml (8 fl oz) vegetable stock and simmer for 20 minutes, or until the vegetables are quite tender. Add 2 sliced courgettes, a 400 g (13 oz) can of chickpeas, drained, 2 tablespoons of honey and 3 tablespoons each of chopped flat-leaf parsley and coriander and cook for a further 10 minutes. Serve with couscous.

sweet & salty couscous 'medfouna'

Serves **6**
Preparation time **20 minutes**
Cooking time **25 minutes**

75 g (3 oz) **butter**
2 tablespoons **sunflower oil**
2 **onions**, finely chopped
2 small **chickens**, cut into
  pieces
1 bunch of **coriander**, chopped
¼ teaspoon **ground ginger**
½ teaspoon **ground turmeric**
pinch of **saffron**
¼ teaspoon **pepper**
100 ml (3½ fl oz) **water**
500 g (1 lb) medium-grain
  couscous
salt
1 tablespoon **cinnamon**,
  to garnish
caster sugar or icing sugar,
  to serve

Melt half the butter and the oil in a heavy-based casserole and soften the onion for 2 minutes.

Add the chicken pieces with the chopped coriander, spices, salt to taste and water. Cook for 20 minutes, stirring from time to time.

When the meat is tender, remove the casserole from the heat, strip the meat from the bones, and mix well with the sauce.

Meanwhile, prepare the couscous following the method on pages 12–13.

Place a third of the couscous on a large serving dish. Spread with half the chicken mixture then cover with another third of the couscous. Spread with the remaining chicken mixture and top with the remaining couscous.

Garnish with the cinnamon and serve with the sugar.

For quick fruit couscous to serve as an accompaniment to meat dishes, bring 500 ml (17 fl oz) chicken or vegetable stock to the boil, then add 50 g (2 oz) each of unsalted butter, chopped fresh or dried dates, chopped dried apricots and sultanas. Boil for 3 minutes, then remove from the heat and add 500 g (1 lb) couscous. Cover and set aside for 5 minutes, then stir in 2–3 teaspoons of cinnamon, to taste, and 50 g (2 oz) toasted flaked almonds.

couscous with buttermilk

Serves **6**
Preparation time **5 minutes**
Cooking time **10 minutes**

500 g (1 lb) medium-grain
 couscous
500 g (1 lb) frozen **broad
 beans**
2 litres (3½ pints) **buttermilk**
pinch of **salt**

Prepare the couscous following the method on pages 12–13.

Meanwhile, cook the broad beans in boiling salted water for 10 minutes.

Separate the couscous grains with your hands, then half-fill bowls with the couscous and pour over the buttermilk. Serve the broad beans separately.

For couscous with yogurt dressing, prepare the couscous and cook the broad beans as above. Place the couscous in a serving bowl with most of the broad beans. Gently fold in a dressing made from 200 g (7 oz) Greek yogurt, 6 tablespoons of water, the finely grated rind and juice of ½ a lemon, 3 tablespoons of chopped coriander, 1 garlic clove crushed with salt and 2 teaspoons of crushed toasted cumin seeds. Serve garnished with the remaining broad beans and some coriander sprigs.

couscous with cinnamon & milk

Serves **6**

Preparation time **5 minutes**

Cooking time **10 minutes**

500 g (1 lb) fine-grain
  couscous

150 g (5 oz) **butter**

1 tablespoon **groundnut oil**

1 tablespoon **cinnamon**, to
  garnish

1 tablespoon **caster sugar**,
  plus extra to serve

1 litre (1¾ pints) **milk**, to
  accompany

Prepare the couscous following the method on pages 12–13, but incorporating the 150 g (5 oz) butter.

Arrange on a serving dish in a cone shape, garnished with the cinnamon and sugar. Serve with milk and extra sugar, to taste.

For couscous with fruit & nuts, stir 50 g (2 oz) each of either muscatel raisins and toasted blanched almonds, Smyrna sultanas and unsalted pistachios, or fresh chopped dates and walnut pieces through the couscous before shaping it into a cone.

pastillas

chicken pastilla

Serves **8**
Preparation time **30 minutes**
Cooking time **45 minutes**

1.5 kg (3 lb) **onions**
2 bunches of **flat-leaf parsley**
200 g (7 oz) **butter**
2 tablespoons **sunflower oil**
1 large **chicken**, weighing
  about 1.8 kg (3½ lb), cut into
  8 pieces
½ teaspoon **ground turmeric**
pinch of **saffron**
½ teaspoon **salt**
½ teaspoon **pepper**
12 **eggs**
1 **lemon**, juiced
1 pack of **filo pastry**
3 tablespoons **plain flour** plus
  2 tablespoons **water**, to seal

Finely mince the onions and parsley. Heat the butter and oil in a heavy-based pan and add the onions, parsley, chicken, spices and half the salt and pepper. When the chicken is cooked, remove the skin and bones and reserve the meat.

Beat the eggs with the remaining salt and pepper and pour into the cooking juices in the pan. Stir rapidly with a wooden spatula and cook until they set. Transfer to a plate and leave to cool. Stir in the lemon juice.

Prepare the pastilla as shown on pages 14–15. Spread the cooled eggs in a thick layer over the base and place the chicken meat on top. Cover with the filo sheets, seal and butter as described. Bake in a preheated oven, 180°C (350°F), Gas Mark 4, for 30 minutes. Serve hot.

For vegetable pastilla, toss 1 kg (2 lb) chopped butternut squash and 250 g (8 oz) quartered shallots in 4 tablespoons of olive oil mixed with 1 teaspoon each of crushed, toasted cumin and coriander seeds, 1 teaspoon each of ground cumin and paprika, ½ teaspoon of ground cinnamon and salt to taste. Cook in a preheated oven, 180°C (350°F), Gas Mark 4, for 20–25 minutes, until golden. Meanwhile, fry 100 g (3½ oz) each of blanched almonds and pistachios with 2 teaspoons of grated root ginger in 1 tablespoon of olive oil until golden, then add 75 g (3 oz) sultanas. Stir in 250 g (8 oz) young spinach and cook until wilted. Add 2 tablespoons of honey, then combine with the roasted vegetables. Complete the pastilla following the steps shown on pages 14–15.

pigeon pastilla

Serves **8**
Preparation time **40 minutes**
Cooking time **45 minutes**

Pastilla
3 large **onions**
2 bunches **flat-leaf parsley**
½ bunch **coriander**
200 g (7 oz) **butter**
3 tablespoons **sunflower oil**
7 **pigeons**, quartered
½ teaspoon **salt**
½ teaspoon **pepper**
1 teaspoon **ground cinnamon**
200 ml (7 fl oz) **water**
12 **eggs**
pinch of **saffron**
¼ teaspoon **turmeric**
250 g (8 oz) blanched
   almonds
100 g (3½ oz) **caster sugar**
1 pack of **filo pastry**
3 tablespoons **plain flour** plus
   2 tablespoons **water**, to seal
100 g (3½ oz) **icing sugar**
   plus 1 tablespoon **cinnamon**,
   to garnish

Finely mince the onions and herbs. Heat the butter and sunflower oil in a heavy-based pan and add the pigeon, onions and herbs, salt, pepper and half the cinnamon. Mix well. Add the water, cover and cook for 15 minutes. Transfer the pigeon pieces to a plate and remove the white meat from the bones (keep the thighs whole).

Beat the eggs with a little salt and pepper, the saffron and the turmeric and pour into the cooking juices in the pan. Stir rapidly with a wooden spatula and cook until they set. Transfer to a plate and leave to cool.

Dry-toast the almonds in a frying pan, then set aside to cool. Once they are cool, crush and mix with the sugar and the remaining cinnamon and set aside.

Prepare the pastilla following the steps on pages 14–15. Spread the cooled eggs in a thick layer over the base and place the pigeon meat on top. Generously sprinkle with the almond, sugar and cinnamon mixture. Cover with the filo sheets, seal and butter as described. Bake in a preheated oven, 180°C (350°F), Gas Mark 4, for 30 minutes.

To serve, sprinkle the top of the pastilla with the icing sugar and use the cinnamon to form intersecting lines.

For pigeon pastilla with ginger, add a 7.5 cm (3 inch) piece of grated fresh root ginger and use a cinnamon stick instead of ground cinnamon in the first step. Reduce the quantity of turmeric added to the beaten eggs to a large pinch.

fish & prawn pastilla

Serves **8**

Preparation time **15 minutes**, plus marinating time

Cooking time **45 minutes**

1 kg (2 lb) **white fish fillets**

500 g (1 lb) raw **prawns**, shelled and deveined

1 bunch of **coriander**, chopped

1 bunch of **flat-leaf parsley**, chopped

3 **garlic cloves**, finely minced

1 tablespoon **paprika**

pinch of **cayenne pepper**

½ teaspoon **ground cumin**

pinch of **mace**

¼ teaspoon **salt**

¼ teaspoon **pepper**

2 tablespoons **white wine vinegar**

50 g (2 oz) **butter**

2 tablespoons **olive oil**

1 large bowl of fine **Chinese noodles**, soaked

1 pack of **filo pastry**

3 tablespoons **plain flour** plus 2 tablespoons **water**, to seal

Put the fish and prawns in a large bowl with the herbs, garlic, spices, salt and pepper and vinegar. Cover with clingfilm and refrigerate for 1 hour.

Melt the butter in a heavy-based casserole, add the oil, and cook the fish and prawns until the flesh begins to flake. Stir in the soaked noodles and cook for 10 minutes over low heat.

Preheat the oven to 180°C (350°F), Gas Mark 4.

Prepare the pastilla following the steps on pages 14–15. Spread the filling in a thick layer over the base. Cover with the filo sheets, seal and butter as described.

Transfer to the oven and bake for 30 minutes.

For fish pastilla with squid, replace 500 g (1 lb) of the white fish fillets with 500 g (1 lb) squid, cleaned and cut into large pieces. Remove the squid pieces from the marinade, cut them into smaller pieces and quickly cook them in the butter and oil until just opaque, then remove from the pan and set aside while you cook the white fish and prawns. Return to the pan with the soaked noodles and complete the recipe as above.

pastilla with custard

Serves **8**
Preparation time **30 minutes**
Cooking time **20 minutes**

Pastilla
250 g (8 oz) blanched
  almonds
50 g (2 oz) **caster sugar**
20 sheets of **filo pastry**
sunflower oil, for frying

Custard
4 **egg yolks**
150 g (5 oz) **caster sugar**
1 tablespoon **vanilla sugar**
2 tablespoons **plain flour**
750 ml (1 ¼ pints) boiling **milk**

To decorate
4 **egg whites**
150 g (5 oz) **caster sugar**
1 tablespoon **water**

Dry-toast the almonds, then set aside to cool. Once cold, roughly chop and mix with the caster sugar.

Put the egg yolks for the custard in a saucepan with the sugars and beat to dissolve. Incorporate the flour, then pour in the boiling milk, beating vigorously over a low heat until the custard thickens. Allow to cool.

Beat the egg whites with 50 g (2 oz) of the caster sugar until stiff. Cook spoonfuls of the meringue mixture in boiling water and set aside.

Fold the filo pastry sheets in four, fan fashion, and fry them in the sunflower oil, a few at a time, then drain on kitchen paper. Place four of the pastry fans on a round plate to form a circle, then add a second layer. Spread with half the cold custard and sprinkle over a third of the almonds. Repeat to make another layer, then top with the remaining four fans.

Decorate with the meringue and sprinkle with the remaining almonds. Quickly prepare a caramel with the remaining caster sugar and the tablespoon of water. Drizzle over the pastilla and serve immediately.

For 'ktefa', prepare the recipe as above, omitting the meringues and caramel and adding 2 teaspoons of orange-flower water to the custard before leaving it to cool. Spread each of the first two layers of pastry fans with a third of the custard, then spread the remaining third on the top layer of pastry fans. Sprinkle with almonds and ground cinnamon before serving.

desserts & sweet things

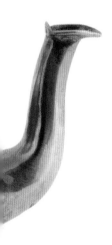

orange salad

Serves **6**
Preparation time **10 minutes**

8 **oranges**
1 tablespoon **icing sugar**
¼ teaspoon **cinnamon**
50 g (2 oz) blanched **almonds**,
   to decorate

Peel 7 of the oranges, removing most of the white pith with the rind. Cut them into 1 cm (½ inch) thick rounds and arrange on a serving plate.

Sprinkle with sugar and squeeze over the juice of the remaining orange.

Sprinkle with cinnamon and decorate with the almonds.

For mixed fruit salad, mix the juice of 2 oranges with 3 tablespoons of honey and 1½ teaspoons of orange-flower water in a serving bowl. Add 250 g (8 oz) each of chopped nectarines, apricots and mangoes, stirring the fruit into the orange and honey dressing as you add it to prevent discolouration. Marinate for 1 hour and serve at room temperature, sprinkled with pomegranate seeds and fresh mint sprigs.

squash preserve

Preparation time **15 minutes**
Cooking time **20 minutes**

1 kg (2 lb) **red-fleshed
squash or pumpkin**, peeled
weight
750 g (1½ lb) **caster sugar**
1 **lemon**, juiced
1 tablespoon **cinnamon**

Remove the seeds and fibre from the squash and dice
the flesh very small. Drop into boiling water and cook
for 5 minutes.

Drain the squash. Tip into a large saucepan, sprinkle
over the sugar and pour in the lemon juice. Cook over a
low heat for 15 minutes, gently stirring from time to time.

Stir in the cinnamon at the end of cooking.

For pumpkin pastilla, blanch 1 kg (2 lb) peeled
pumpkin chunks in boiling water for 10 minutes. Drain,
then cook in 50 g (2 oz) butter over a low heat for
30 minutes, stirring occasionally. Mash to a purée, then
stir in 50 g (2 oz) sugar, 2 tablespoons of honey, a
pinch of saffron, ½ teaspoon each of ground ginger and
cinnamon and ¼ teaspoon of salt and cook, stirring, until
the purée is dry and firm. Remove from the heat and
stir in 250 g (8 oz) chopped walnuts. Mix 150 g (5 oz)
icing sugar with 200 g (7 oz) toasted flaked almonds,
¼ teaspoon of ground cinnamon and 2 tablespoons of
orange-flower water. Prepare the pastilla (see pages
14–15) and fill with the pumpkin purée topped with
the almond mixture. Cook in a preheated oven, 180°C
(350°F), Gas Mark 4, for 30 minutes, or until golden.
Serve sprinkled with icing sugar and ground cinnamon.

candied oranges

Soaking time **12 hours**
Preparation time **20 minutes**
Cooking time **20 minutes**

1.5 kg (3 lb) **navel oranges**
1 kg (2 lb) **caster sugar**
1 **lemon**, juiced
¼ teaspoon **salt**

Select thick-skinned oranges. Grate them to remove the rind, then place the oranges in a bowl of salted water and leave to soak overnight.

Rinse the oranges under plenty of running water, then bring to the boil in a saucepan of water. As soon as the water boils, remove and drain the oranges. Cut into quarters or sixths, depending on size.

Place the pieces in a preserving pan, cover with sugar, pour in the lemon juice and cook over a low heat, gently turning the pieces once to avoid damaging them.

Once the oranges are a rich golden colour and the syrup has reduced, remove from the heat and arrange in serving dishes.

For candied lemon peel to serve with coffee, peel 6 thick-skinned, unwaxed lemons in lengthways quarters. Scrape off most of the white pith. Place the peel in a pan, cover with cold water, then bring to the boil and blanch for 1 minute. Drain and repeat, then slice the peel into thin strips. Bring 500 ml (17 fl oz) water to the boil with 500 g (1 lb) sugar and simmer for 45 minutes. Stir the lemon peel strips into the syrup and simmer for 10 minutes. Leave to cool in the syrup overnight, then drain. Working in batches, toss the strips in sugar until coated, then spread them out on baking sheets to dry. Store in the refrigerator in an airtight jar.

aubergine preserve

Soaking time **12 hours**
Preparation time **10 minutes**
Cooking time **45 minutes**

1 kg (2 lb) very small
  aubergines
1 kg (2 lb) **granulated sugar**
200 ml (7 fl oz) **water**
1 **lemon**, juiced
5 or 6 **cloves**
¼ teaspoon **mixed spice**
2 small pieces **gum arabic**
salt

Prick the aubergines all over with a fork. Place them in a large bowl of salted water and leave to soak overnight.

Rinse the aubergines in plenty of running water, then drop into boiling water and cook for 10 minutes. Drain and set aside.

Put the sugar into a large saucepan with the water and allow to dissolve slowly. Pour in the lemon juice, then add the spices, gum arabic and the drained aubergines. Once the aubergines have absorbed the sugar, turn off the heat and drain.

For fresh fig preserve, place 1 kg (2 lb) quartered fresh figs in a pan with 150 g (5 oz) sugar, 300 ml (10 fl oz) water and the finely grated rind and juice of 1 lemon. Slowly bring to the boil, then simmer over a low heat, stirring occasionally, for about 1½ hours or until the figs are cooked and the preserve has thickened.

sultana & walnut preserve 'mrozia'

Preparation time **5 minutes**
Cooking time **50 minutes**

1 kg (2 lb) large **sultanas**
200 g (7 oz) **caster sugar**
¼ teaspoon **ground cinnamon**
2 tablespoons **groundnut oil**
200 ml (7 fl oz) **water**
500 g (1 lb) **walnuts**

Rinse the sultanas and place in a large saucepan with the sugar, cinnamon, oil and water.

Cook over a very low heat for around 45 minutes, stirring from time to time; the sultanas should not be too coloured.

Meanwhile, dry-toast the walnuts over a low heat for 5 minutes, then remove and leave to cool. When they are cold, roughly crush them in your hand and add them to the sultanas 5 minutes before the end of cooking.

Tip into a preserving jar and leave to cool.

For fig & walnut preserve, replace the sultanas with 500 g (1 lb) each of raisins and chopped dried figs (trim and discard the stalks). Replace the cinnamon with 2 teaspoons of ras-el-hanout.

preserved clementines

Soaking time **12 hours**
Preparation time **10 minutes**
Cooking time **2 hours**

1 kg (2 lb) small **clementines**
1 kg (2 lb) **sugar**
1 **lemon**, juiced
1 litre (1¾ pints) **water**

Place the clementines in a bowl of water and leave to soak overnight.

Pierce the fruit from top to bottom and on all sides with a skewer.

Place the clementines in a large saucepan, sprinkle with sugar and lemon juice, and pour in the water. Leave the sugar to dissolve over low heat.

Cook for a total of 2 hours, in three or four stages, allowing the fruit to cool between each stage.

For clementine cake, process 300 g (10 oz) well-drained preserved clementines to a fairly coarse purée in a food processor. Transfer to a mixing bowl and stir in 5 tablespoons of sunflower oil, 3 tablespoons of argan oil, 200 ml (7 fl oz) milk and 50 g (2 oz) honey. Sift together 225 g (7½ oz) plain flour with 1½ teaspoons of baking powder, 2 teaspoons of bicarbonate of soda and ¼ teaspoon of salt and fold into the clementine mixture. Pour into a greased and lined cake tin and cook in a preheated oven, 180°C (350°F), Gas Mark 4, for about 45 minutes, or until just firm to the touch.

caramelized nuts

Preparation time **10 minutes**
Cooking time **15 minutes**

150 g (5 oz) unblanched
almonds or pistachios
100 g (3½ oz) **caster sugar**
1 tablespoon **groundnut oil**

Heat a nonstick frying pan over very low heat.

Add the almonds or pistachios and sugar and allow the sugar to melt, stirring from time to time with a wooden spatula until the sugar turns to caramel.

Oil a baking tray with the groundnut oil, then use a spoon to remove a few nuts and form into a small pile on the tray. Repeat with all the nuts.

Once the nuts are cold, transfer from the tray to a serving plate.

For caramelized sesame seeds, add 150 g (5 oz) of white sesame seeds and 200 g (7 oz) caster sugar to a nonstick frying pan over a very low heat. Allow the sugar to melt and caramelize as above. Tip the mixture into an oiled baking tray and flatten the surface with a rolling pin. Cut into small pieces while still hot and soft.

almond 'ghoriba'

Makes around **30**
Preparation time **20 minutes**
Cooking time **20 minutes**

1 kg (2 lb) blanched **almonds**,
  plus a few extra, to decorate
500 g (1 lb) **icing sugar**
½ tablespoon **baking powder**
3 tablespoons melted **butter**
6 **egg yolks**
2 **whole eggs**
rind of 1 **lemon**
150 ml (¼ pint) **orange-flower**
  water

Preheat the oven to 180°C (350°F), Gas Mark 4.

Finely chop the almonds in a blender.

Tip the almonds into a mixing bowl and mix in two-thirds of the icing sugar, the baking powder, butter, egg yolks and whole eggs, and lemon rind.

Add the orange-flower water to make a dough. Using wetted hands, form into balls about the size of a walnut.

Tip the remaining icing sugar onto a plate and roll each ball in it until coated. Place on an oiled baking sheet, spaced well apart. Press an almond into the top of each one and transfer to the oven. Cook for 15 minutes.

For speedy almond 'ghoriba', place 600 g (1 lb 3½ oz) ground almonds in a food processor with 225 g (7½ oz) caster sugar, the finely grated rind of 1½ lemons, 3–4 drops of almond essence and 2 medium egg whites. Process to a soft paste. Using wetted hands, form into balls about the size of a walnut. Roll each ball in icing sugar, as above, then place on a greased baking sheet, flattening the balls slightly. Press a blanched almond into the top of each one. Bake in a preheated oven, 200°C (400°F), Gas Mark 6, for 15 minutes.

date crescents

Makes around **40**
Preparation time **30 minutes**
Cooking time **15 minutes**

Pastry
500 g (1 lb) **plain flour**
pinch of **baking powder**
125 g (4 oz) **granulated sugar**
250 g (8 oz) **butter**, melted

Filling
250 g (8 oz) **date paste** (or
   use stoned, chopped dates)
1 knob of **butter**
½ teaspoon **cinnamon**
125 g (4 oz) **icing sugar**

Preheat the oven to 150°C (300°F), Gas Mark 2.

Make the pastry by mixing all the ingredients to form a dough. Leave it to rest while you make the filling.

Mix all the ingredients for the filling and form into balls the size of a hazelnut.

Form the pastry into balls the size of a walnut. Press a ball of filling into each one, close the pastry around it, then fashion it into the shape of a crescent.

Place on an oiled baking sheet and cook for 15 minutes. Remove from the oven and dredge each crescent through the icing sugar to coat on all sides.

For date & nut balls, make the filling from 250 g (8 oz) date paste mixed with 75 g (3 oz) each of chopped walnuts and almonds and 1 teaspoon of vanilla extract. Form into balls the size of a hazelnut. Form the pastry into balls the size of a walnut, press a ball of filling into each one, close the pastry around it and fashion it back into a ball shape. Cook and dredge with icing sugar, as above.

little 'm'hanncha' (moroccan 'snakes')

Makes **10**
Preparation time **30 minutes**
Cooking time **15 minutes**

500 g (1 lb) blanched
  almonds, plus 10 extra to
  decorate
300 g (10 oz) **caster sugar**
5 tablespoons **orange-flower
  water**
1 tablespoon **cinnamon**
150 g (5 oz) **butter**, melted
10 sheets of **filo pastry**
1 beaten **egg**
300 g (10 oz) **honey**

Chop the almonds in a blender, then add the sugar and 1 tablespoon of the orange-flower water and chop again until fine. Tip the mixture into a bowl and add the cinnamon and 50 g (2 oz) of the butter. Mix to a paste and form into 10 rolls, 15 cm (6 inches) long and 2 cm (1 inch) wide. Set aside.

Preheat the oven to 120°C (250°F), Gas Mark ½.

Cut each sheet of filo in two. Brush a half-sheet with melted butter, top with another half-sheet and brush it with butter. With the long edges facing you, fold over a 2.5 cm (1 inch) border and stick with the beaten egg. Place an almond roll along the folded edge and roll up in the filo, then roll the length into a spiral. Repeat with the remaining pastry sheets and rolls of filling. Place on an oiled baking sheet and brush with melted butter. Press a whole almond into the centre of each spiral. Transfer to the oven and cook for 12–15 minutes.

Meanwhile, heat the honey and remaining orange-flower water together.

Dip the cooked cakes, still hot, in the honey mixture and arrange on a serving platter.

For pistachio 'snakes', replace the blanched almonds with blanched pistachios and the orange-flower water with rose water. Reduce the quantity of cinnamon to ½ tablespoon and add the finely ground seeds of two cardamom pods. Use a pale, mild-flavoured honey, such as acacia or clover, for the coating mixture.

gazelle horns

Makes **50**
Preparation time **25 minutes**
Cooking time **15 minutes**

Pastry
300 g (10 oz) **plain flour**
50 g (2 oz) **butter**, softened
4 tablespoons **orange-flower
  water**
2 tablespoons **icing sugar**
pinch of **salt**

Filling
500 g (1 lb) blanched
  almonds
300 g (10 oz) **caster sugar**
1 tablespoon **orange-flower
  water**
25 g (1 oz) **butter**, melted
1 tablespoon **cinnamon**

Rub together the ingredients for the pastry. If it seems too dry, add a little water or extra orange-flower water. Let it rest in the refrigerator while you prepare the filling.

Chop the almonds in a blender, then add the sugar and orange-flower water and chop again until fine. Tip the mixture into a bowl and add the butter and cinnamon. Mix to a dough and form into sticks 8 cm (3½ inches) long.

Preheat the oven to 180°C (350°F), Gas Mark 4.

Divide the pastry into about 50 small balls. Roll out the balls thinly into rectangles and place a stick of almond paste on each one. Close the pastry around the filling, press to seal and trim to form a horn shape. Place them on an oiled baking sheet.

Transfer to the oven and cook for 15 minutes. Allow to cool before serving.

For moroccan mint tea to serve six as an accompaniment, bring 2 litres (1¾ pints) water to the boil. Warm a large teapot with boiling water, then add 3 tablespoons of gunpowder green tea leaves and a little of the measured boiling water. Swish the tea in the water, then strain off the water, leaving the wet tea leaves in the pot. Add the remaining boiling water and allow the tea to steep for 5 minutes, then add 1 bunch of fresh spearmint leaves and steep for a further 5 minutes. Stir in 75 g (3 oz) sugar, then strain the tea and serve garnished with a mint sprig.

pistachio baklavas

Baklavas
300 g (10 oz) raw **pistachio
  nuts**
100 g (3½ oz) **sugar**
1 tablespoon **orange-flower
  water**
8 sheets of **filo pastry**
1 **egg white**
100 g (3½ oz) **butter**, melted

Glaze
250 g (8 oz) **honey**
2 tablespoons **orange-flower
  water**

Dry-roast the nuts in a medium-hot oven for 15 minutes, then rub off the skins and finely chop with the sugar. Add the orange-flower water, then set the mixture aside.

Take 2 filo pastry sheets, overlap slightly on the long sides, and stick them together with egg white. Butter generously, then fold in the top and bottom edges to form a rectangle. Place a quarter of the filling in the centre, fold the pastry sheet over into the centre then again to bring in the sides, flattening slightly to make a parcel around 5 cm (2 inches) wide. Repeat to make a total of four long parcels. Place on a tray, cover with clingfilm and place a weight on top. Leave overnight.

Preheat the oven to 150°C (300°F), Gas Mark 2.

Unwrap the cakes and place them in a buttered baking tin. Slice each cake into six pieces on the diagonal, using a very sharp knife. Do not separate them completely. Transfer the tin to the oven and cook for 20 minutes.

Meanwhile, heat the honey with the orange-flower water for the glaze. Immediately the baklavas are cooked, coat them with the hot glaze. Leave to stand for 1 hour before removing them from the tin.

For dates stuffed with pistachios, place 200 g (7 oz) blanched pistachios in a food processor with 100 g (3½ oz) icing sugar and 2 tablespoons of orange-flower water and process to a paste. Make a slit in one side of each date and press in a small knob of paste (this quantity will fill about 500 g/1 lb fresh dates).

moroccan rice pudding

Serves **6**
Preparation time **5 minutes**
Cooking time **40 minutes**

300 g (10 oz) **short-grain rce**
1 knob of **butter**
2 litres (3½ pints) **milk**
200 g (7 oz) **caster sugar**
½ teaspoon **salt**
1 tablespoon **orange-flower water**

Cook the rice following the packet instructions. Once the water has been completely absorbed, add the butter, milk, sugar and salt.

Bring back to the boil, stirring from time to time so that the rice does not stick, then add the orange-flower water, and continue to stir until the milk has the consistency of custard.

Remove from the heat and continue to stir to prevent a skin from forming. Serve in a large bowl.

For rice pudding with almond milk, blend 25 g (1 oz) chopped blanched almonds in a food processor or blender with 4 tablespoons of boiling water. Push the mixture through a fine sieve into a bowl, then blend with another 4 tablespoons of boiling water and sieve again. Pour into a measuring jug and make up to 2 litres (3½ pints) with milk. Complete the recipe as above.

honey halva 'griwach'

Makes **20**
Preparation time **30 minutes**
Cooking time **15 minutes**

Halva
150 g (5 oz) **white sesame
  seeds**
1 packet fast-action **dried
  yeast**
1 kg (2 lb) **plain flour**
4 teaspoons **baking powder**
½ teaspoon **ground turmeric**
pinch of **saffron**
350 ml of a mixture of melted
  butter and sunflower oil
3 tablespoons **vinegar**
oil, for frying

Glaze
375 ml (13 fl oz) runny **honey**
150 ml (¼ pint) **orange-flower
  water**

Dry-roast the sesame seeds in a frying pan over a low heat. Remove and leave to cool.

Mix the yeast in a bowl with a little warm water. Tip the flour into a large bowl, make a hollow in the centre and add in all the other ingredients except the oil. Knead the dough thoroughly, then roll out and cut into 10 x 8 cm (4 x 3½ inches) rectangles, 2.5 cm (1 inch) thick. Twist the rectangles and join the two ends.

Heat the oil in a deep-fat fryer or deep-sided frying pan and fry the cakes in batches until golden on all sides.

Meanwhile, heat the honey with the orange-flower water. Dip the hot halva in the glaze, then sprinkle with the sesame seeds.

For baked halva, beat 125 g (4 oz) butter with 125 g (4 oz) caster sugar, then add 175 g (6 oz) fine semolina, 2 teaspoons of baking powder, 125 g (4 oz) ground almonds, the finely grated rind and juice of 1 small orange and 3 large eggs. Beat until smooth. Bake in a greased and lined 23 cm (9 inch) square cake tin in a preheated oven, 220°C (425°F), Gas Mark 7, for 20 minutes until golden and almost firm. Meanwhile, place 175 g (6 oz) caster sugar, 275 ml (9 fl oz) water, 1 cinnamon stick broken in half and strips of rind from 1 orange in a pan. Heat gently, stirring, to dissolve the sugar; boil without stirring for 5 minutes. Remove from the heat, discard the cinnamon and orange rind, and stir in the juice of ½ lemon and 2 tablespoons of orange-flower water. Prick all over with a skewer and pour over the syrup. Serve cold.

moroccan pancakes

Makes around **20**
Preparation time **20 minutes**,
  plus resting
Cooking time **20 minutes**

500 g (1 lb) **bread flour**
150 g (5 oz) **ground wheat or
  fine semolina**
½ packet fast-action **dried
  yeast**
½ teaspoon **salt**
200 ml (7 fl oz) tepid **water**
100 g (3½ oz) **butter**, melted
5 tablespoons **groundnut oil**
sugar or **honey**, to serve

Mix together all the dry ingredients in a large bowl and add the water little by little, working it in until you have a very supple dough. Allow it to rest for 5 minutes.

Divide the dough into pieces the size of a tennis ball and place them on an oiled worktop. Leave to rest for a further 5 minutes.

Melt the butter and mix with the oil. Coat your hands in the mixture and, taking each ball in turn, stretch the dough into a large, very thin, almost transparent, disc.

Coat your hands again in the butter and oil mixture, fold the discs in three, then into three again to form a square, tuck in the ends, and leave to rest for 10 minutes.

Cook each parcel in a hot frying pan for 1 minute, turning over halfway through. Serve hot, with either sugar or honey.

For yeast-free moroccan pancakes, sift 500 g (1 lb) plain flour into a bowl with a pinch of salt. Gradually add 125–150 ml (about ¼ pint) water and, using your hands, work the flour into the liquid until the mixture comes together into a smooth, not sticky, dough. Divide the dough into 20 pieces and roll each into a ball. Complete the recipe as above and serve warm, with honey.

baghrir

Makes **12**
Preparation time **10 minutes**, plus resting
Cooking time **12 minutes**

150 g (5 oz) **plain flour**
500 g (1 lb) fine **semolina**
4 **eggs**
1 litre (1¾ pints) **milk**
40 g (1½ oz) **yeast**
½ teaspoon **salt**
honey, to serve

Blend all the ingredients except the honey in a food processor and leave to rest for 1 hour.

Lightly grease a heavy frying pan or crêpe pan with a drop of oil and place over a medium heat.

Pour a ladleful of batter into the pan, spread thinly and leave to cook for 1 minute without turning. Remove from the heat once the surface of the bghrir is full of holes. Continue to cook the bghrir until all the batter is used up.

Serve with honey.

For semolina 'soup' with milk & honey, bring 1.5 litres (2½ pints) water to the boil. Stir in 200 g (7 oz) coarse semolina and 1 teaspoon of salt. Gently simmer over a low heat, stirring, for about 15 minutes or until the semolina is cooked and the mixture has thickened. Stir in 1 litre (1¾ pints) milk, 50 g (2 oz) butter and 1½ teaspoons of ground aniseed. Bring back to a simmer and cook for a further 10 minutes, until thickened. Stir in 4–6 tablespoons of honey, to taste, and serve drizzled with a little extra honey.

fromage blanc with honey

Makes around **12**

Serves **6**

Preparation time **10 minutes**, plus resting

1 litre (2 pints) **whey**
500 ml (1 pint) whole **milk**
¼ teaspoon **salt**

7 **walnut halves** and
1 tablespoon **honey**, to serve

Pour the whey into a mixing bowl.

Pour the milk and the salt into a saucepan and bring to the boil, then pour onto the whey, beating with a hand whisk. Cover and leave to rest for 12 hours.

Drain the mixture through a fine muslin cloth placed in a large colander until the cheese has firmed up.

Turn the cheese into a serving dish, decorate with the walnuts and drizzle with the honey.

For pomegranate seeds with orange-flower water
to serve as an accompaniment, mix the seeds from 6 pomegranates with 4½ tablespoons of sugar and 3 tablespoons of orange-flower water and stir gently to combine. Sprinkle with a little ground cinnamon to serve.

index

acknowledgements

Special photography by Michel Reuss.

Other photographs © **Octopus Publishing
Group** David Munns 85, 87; Ian Wallace 39,
41, 113, 155, 163, 173; Lis Parsons 49, 95, 97,
109, 151, 153, 177; Sean Myers 77; Stephen
Conroy 101, 127; William Lingwood 93; William
Reavell 65; William Shaw 115. © **Shutterstock**
Philip Lange 2–3; Kippy Lanker 4–5; Eric
Gevaert 6–7; Miljan Petrovic 16–17; Bogdan
Ionescu 58–59, 186–187; Laurent Renault
70–71; Monkey Business Images 116–117;
Nicobatista 140–141; Peter D. 156–157;
Hamiza Bakirci 170–171; Farres 196–197;
Inacio Pires 232–233.

Executive Editor: Eleanor Maxfield
Managing Editor: Clare Churly
Senior Art Editor: Juliette Norsworthy
Translation, editing and design: JMS Book LLP
Picture Library Manager: Jennifer Veall
Senior Production Controller: Caroline Alberti